Items should be returned on or before the last ⌐
shown below. Items not already requested by ⌐
borrowers may be renewed in person, in writing or by
telephone. To renew, please quote the number on the
barcode label. To renew online a PIN is required.
This can be requested at your local library.
Renew online @ www.dublincitypubliclibraries.ie
Fines charged for overdue items will include postage
incurred in recovery. Damage to or loss of items will
be charged to the borrower.

Leabharlanna Poiblí Chathair Bhaile Átha Cliath
Dublin City Public Libraries

Dublin City
Baile Átha Cliath

Date Due	Date Due	Date Due
13. FEB 08	- 3 AUG 2012	- 9 JUN 2016
	2 2 NOV 2013	Withdrawn from Stock
05. MAR. 09	E 6 SEP 2014	Dublin City Public Libraries
1 0 FEB 2010	0 3 NOV 2015	
2 5 MAY 2011		
1 2 MAR 2012	0 3 FEB 2016	Withdrawn from Stock Dublin City Public Libraries

C▲R
basics

Kevin Elliott

First published in 2004 by HarperCollins*Publishers*
77–85 Fulham Palace Road, London, W6 8JB

The Collins website address is:
www.collins.co.uk

Text by Kevin Elliott; copyright © HarperCollins*Publishers*
Artworks and design © HarperCollins*Publishers*
Photography by Kevin Elliott and Focus Publishing

Conceived and created by: **Focus Publishing**, Sevenoaks, Kent
Project editor: Guy Croton
Editor: Vanessa Townsend
Project co-ordinator: Caroline Watson
Design & illustration: David Etherington

For HarperCollins
Senior managing editor: Angela Newton
Design manager: Luke Griffin
Editor: Alastair Laing
Editorial assistant: Lisa John
Production: Chris Gurney

A CIP catalogue record for this book is available from the British Library
ISBN 0007175515

Colour reproduction by Colourscan
Printed and bound by Scotprint

CONTENTS

INTRODUCTION

If car ownership – or potential car ownership – is new to you, there is an awful lot you will want to know about the subject before you jump in at the deep end and buy a vehicle.

Even if you are one of the many people who have been driving for a while, you may still want to know more about the subject.

Owning a car can be a scary proposition at times: it is all very well while everything is running smoothly, but what would you do if a headlight bulb stopped working or a red light on the dashboard came on and glared at you, spelling O-I-L? Does the thought of having to deal with the salesman at your local dealer scare you or do you sometimes wonder what you would do if you broke down? The book you have in your hands will lead you through all these predicaments – and more – with honest, practical and sensible advice and clear guidance.

This book is not intended to be a heavyweight, hands-on guide to fixing your car – there are plenty of manuals available covering individual models that do that – but we will show you how to undertake basic tasks such as changing the battery, fitting new light bulbs, checking the fluids and changing a wheel. Basically, we cover all the essential information you need to keep your car on the road, but nothing as complex or demanding as doing your own servicing or major maintenance.

Whether you are young or old, male or female, a novice or an experienced motorist, there is always something new you can learn about owning and driving your car.

If you want to modify your car, maximise its capacity or enhance its practicality, the following chapters will give you the advice you need.

What we will also show you is how to go about buying a car – either new or second-hand; how to prepare, present and sell a car; and everything in between. *Collins Car Basics* also includes where and why your car should have an MOT test and how to get it to pass; a guide to all the legal paperwork that you need when you own a car; safety and security; and what to do in the unfortunate event of an accident.

Apart from taking on a mortgage, buying a car can be the biggest single expenditure a person is likely to make. Therefore you will want to know you have got the right car for you, as well as knowing how to take care of it and prevent it from being stolen or broken into. *Collins Car Basics* is the perfect size to keep in your glovebox, so you can pull it out and refer to it exactly when and

where you need it. There is no point in explaining how to change a wheel if the book is at home and you are miles from anywhere with a flat tyre.

This book will show you the basics of car ownership and maintenance, so hopefully you will gain confidence on the road. But you can help yourself, too. Carrying a mobile telephone (though not using it while driving, as that is an offence), and joining one of the motoring organisations that offer breakdown assistance and recovery, are definitely two of the best moves you can make for peace of mind. They are invaluable in the event of an accident or breakdown. Just knowing help is at hand or on its way makes a big difference, especially to lone or inexperienced drivers. Hopefully, however, some of the advice in this book will help you to get back on the road unaided.

Whether you read this book from cover to cover or just search for answers whenever you need to know something, *Collins Car Basics* is an indispensable guide to all the questions you may have about cars, and some you won't have thought of yet. You won't find any assumptions that you know anything about cars

It doesn't matter if your car is new or old, large or small, this book will help you run it better.

already, but you will find plenty of advice, tips and 'dos and don'ts', contact numbers and website addresses. All of these are designed to help you save money on your motoring, keep safe and stay legal.

1

£15,99

SOLD

Choosing a car can be a minefield. Your selection will depend on budget and lifestyle, but may also be influenced by a clear preference for a certain type or look of vehicle. This chapter will help you consider the numerous options and define your ultimate choice.

CHOOSING A NEW CAR TO SUIT YOU

There are numerous points to consider when buying a new car. For instance, will you use it for long journeys? What size car do you need? Will you regularly carry passengers? What is your budget?

Your motoring priorities will dictate what kind of car you look for. For example, is cheap reliable transport your major concern, or does high specification and luxury appeal to you? This is where your budget will influence your decision. You cannot buy a Mercedes for Ford Fiesta money.

If small children are going to use the car often, then a four door would be best. Check that the rear doors have child safety locks, so they cannot be opened from the inside. If you rarely carry passengers, and never more than one, but often have to park in confined spaces, something like a Mini or Smart car may be most practical for you. Will the car be the sole means of transport for you and your family? If so, make sure the interior is large enough and comfortable for everyone.

If high mileages are to be expected, consider buying a diesel powered car for economy. Modern diesels are almost indistinguishable from petrol powered cars in their driving manner, yet offer savings in running costs if used frequently.

Do your homework for the car you prefer before walking into a showroom.

Families will generally opt for a four or five door model for the sake of practicality.

What will your car be used for? Will it be tackling the school run twice a day and not much else, or will it be constantly in use? If it will be carrying more than just people around, you may find a hatchback will offer you more practicality than a regular saloon car with a boot. Hatchbacks cover not just the small car 'supermini' genre but smaller mid-sized cars such as the Ford Focus and even some smaller MPVs (Multi Purpose Vehicles or 'people carriers').

You may want to look at resale values, as some cars depreciate far quicker than others. If you plan on keeping the car for a few years this may not seem so important now, but it is worth checking. Do some homework, too, when it comes to running costs. What is the fuel consumption? Also, get

a few insurance quotes before parting with any money, as you may find that the cost of covering the model you are interested in is simply too high. If you really want a certain car, choose a lower specification in the same bodystyle to secure a smaller insurance premium.

It is also important to check the warranty level on offer. Warranties vary greatly, depending on the manufacturer. Some manufacturers now offer warranties as long as five years.

AUTO ADVICE

Arrange to take any models you are interested in for a test drive, making this an extended drive in the case of your final choice.

CHOOSING A SECOND-HAND CAR

All the points on the previous pages are as relevant to second-hand cars as they are to new cars, but when it comes to buying a used car you have more options and should be much more wary.

Ideally, always opt for a used car that is less than two years old, which will usually come from leasing companies and rental fleets, sourced from a car supermarket or a dealer approved scheme. In this instance it is likely that the car's warranty will still be valid, and it will have undergone regular servicing and maintenance. It may have high mileage, but modern cars are perfectly capable of well over 100,000 miles with regular servicing. A high mileage car used mainly on motorways will often be a better bet

Opt for the youngest used car that you can afford – two to three years is a good objective.

than a low mileage car that has been used primarily around town.

When you buy a second-hand car, you have far more choice over buying a new car, in that you have many more models to choose from within your budget. Buying a used

AUTO ADVICE

Although private sales can be more risky, you can pick up decent bargains if you are thorough in all your checks.

car quite often means that more luxurious cars of a better specification will fall into your price range as well. You also have more choice in that you can buy used cars from more outlets than new cars. Recognised dealers, auctions, car supermarkets, small traders and even private sellers will all have something to offer.

Car supermarkets offer great choice and very keen prices, but they will almost certainly refuse to haggle and tend to offer very low prices for part exchanges. Buying from a recognised dealer is probably the safest bet, but they usually have the highest prices. Approved used car schemes through dealers do offer peace of mind, however, and often include a warranty and a thorough pre-sales check. Private sales can provide the best bargains but can also be risky. There is very little legal protection if you buy a car this way, and this could be important if the car turns out to be stolen or have outstanding finance owed on it. If you

Trade magazines or newspaper ads are a good source to find a used car.

choose to buy privately, always inspect the Registration Document and check its details against the vehicle.

Wherever you opt to buy a car, find one with minimal faults. Check the paintwork, as damaged paint will accelerate rust. Find out what is on offer with the car, such as a warranty, inspection or history check, and read the small print for exclusions. Have the car independently inspected (see page 19) and have a history check carried out (see page 20), for peace of mind.

If you have a problem with a used car, unless it was bought privately you have some redress under the 1979 Sale of Goods Act.

car buying dos & don'ts

▸ **DO** get insurance quotes before buying, as well as checking running costs (see www.glass.co.uk), to ensure that you can afford to run the car.

▸ **DON'T** let a private seller bring the car to you – always visit them.

▸ **DO** look at several cars before buying.

WHAT TO LOOK OUT FOR

You have found the make and model of car that seems perfect for you. But first appearances can be deceptive. Here are a few pointers to ensure you have made a wise – and prudent – choice.

With a brand new car there should be no need to perform any checks on the condition of the vehicle. However, you should sit inside the car, make sure you are comfortable in the driving position, check that visibility is good and you can reach all the pedals. Sit the family in the car as well, just to ensure that there is enough room for them all. Check the luggage space will be large enough for anything you are likely to carry with you, such as pushchairs, toys or maybe bicycles. Can the seats be folded easily if this is something you do regularly?

Take the car on a long test drive – some dealers allow 24 hour or weekend tests – and if you are going to be using the car for extended motorway driving, test that too, even if it is only on a dual carriageway. Check for wind, engine and road noise, and how well the car responds when overtaking. Drive the car on as many different road surfaces as you can and decide whether you are happy with the suspension, steering, power and gear change. If you are not happy, or some aspect of the car irritates you, will you be able to live with it on a long-term basis?

CHECK IT OUT

When viewing used cars there are more checks you should make, though this does depend on where you are buying the car.

Take the car out for a thorough test run, so that you can experience exactly how it drives.

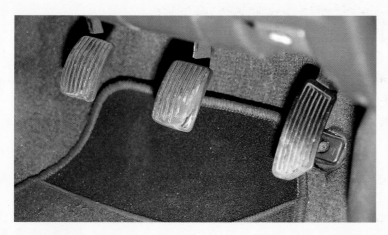

Worn pedal rubbers are a common sign that the car has been well used. Check the mileage carefully if you see excessive wear on the pedals.

A nearly new car from a dealer or supermarket should not need as detailed a check as a car offered by a private seller. The dealer is under an obligation to offer goods that are free from defects – unless they are brought to your attention by him. Assume, for the following checks, that the vehicle is offered for sale privately. This way we will cover all the checks and you can decide whether they are necessary for your own situation.

One of the golden rules of buying a car is never to view it in the dark or in the rain. You will simply not see mismatched paint, bodywork damage or the general condition of the car this way. High mileage cars will have telltale signs like worn pedal rubbers and carpet underneath them, and most likely a worn driver's seat. Does one key operate all the doors, boot and the ignition? It

should do, so if not, ask why. Are the tyres in good condition? Check the bodywork for damage, and if it shows signs of recent paintwork, such as paint on handles or door and window rubber seals, again ask why. Was it rusty or damaged?

Some unscrupulous traders will repair accident damaged or, even worse, written-off cars (when a car is too badly damaged after an accident to be repaired or when it would be uneconomical to do so) and resell them without declaring their history.

AUTO ADVICE
If you are unsure whether the car's mileage is genuine, quite often there are tell-tale signs in the condition of the car.

Some may even be 'cut and shut'. This is where the front half of one car is joined to the rear half of another. Done properly, this can make for a bodyshell

Start the engine and check the exhaust for excessive or blue coloured smoke.

car checks dos & don'ts

▶ **DO** check the identification number of the vehicle against the Registration Document.

▶ **DON'T** buy a car if you are not happy with its condition – there are plenty of other cars on the market!

▶ **DO** look at the vehicle's panels, especially in the engine bay, to see whether there is any damage or any obvious signs of repair.

▶ **DON'T** ever view a car in the dark or when it is raining.

▶ **DO** start the engine up and listen for any unusual noises, then check the exhaust for excessive or blue smoke.

no weaker than the original, but most such jobs are done badly! The front half of the car is where the identification plate is normally located, so this half is the new identity of the vehicle. However, the back could be newer or older, depending on the model. Some manufacturers now stamp the identification number in various places around the car, which makes this practice harder to detect. Suffice to say, if you think you have come across a 'cut and shut' car, NEVER buy it.

Open the bonnet and check the inner panels, especially at the front of the engine bay, for damage or signs of repair. Most accident damaged

AUTO ADVICE

Although most private vendors are trustworthy, you should always carry out thorough checks.

cars suffer damage at the front, and though outer panels are replaced easily, inner structural panels are harder to change. Check the engine for any obvious fluid leaks. Start the engine, listen for any unusual noises and check the exhaust for excessive smoke. Blue smoke can signify a worn engine, while white smoke or steam can be caused by water getting into the engine. It can also be caused by condensation in the exhaust pipe, so wait to see if it clears after a minute or so.

Take the car for a drive – ensuring that your own, or the vendor's, insurance covers you

before doing so – and carefully observe the operation of the brakes, steering and gearbox. Check the car doesn't pull to one side while braking, and that the steering is smooth and not 'notchy'. Gear selection should feel smooth and positive. Are there any unusual vibrations while the car is in motion? Do all the instruments work?

If you are happy with the condition, ask to see the Registration Document and check the details against vendor and the vehicle. Open up the bonnet. Usually, a plate on the panel beside the bonnet catch shows the car's VIN (Vehicle Identification Number). This should match the number on the Registration Document, as should the registration number. If the vendor has no Registration Document, go no further. Think hard, also, if the car seems cheap and the vendor seems anxious to sell. The car may well be stolen. It pays to be cautious.

It is important that the vehicle's identification number matches its registration document.

GETTING YOUR CAR INSPECTED

Having an independent expert inspect a car before purchase is a good idea, even if the car has been inspected by a dealer and is being sold with a warranty or service contract.

An independent report on a car's condition may highlight any faults and enable you to negotiate a better price, but more importantly it will bring to light any vehicle in an unroadworthy condition. Pre-purchase vehicle inspections are carried out by a number of companies – type 'vehicle inspections', 'car inspections' or 'car inspection services' into an internet search engine for a list – or by motoring organisations such as the AA (0800 085 3007) and RAC (0870 533 3660). Most independent companies offer nationwide inspections and one,

Used Car Checks (08700 46 86 02), even offers a warranty from the UK's largest independent warranty company.

Whether you use a motoring organisation or independent company, they will inspect the vehicle and give you a report on its condition. The vehicle is inspected for faults or repairs to either mechanical components or bodywork that is below standard. Once the bodywork, underside and engine have been inspected, the car is taken for a road test. Clarify with the company what is and is not checked, and inform them of the vehicle to be checked, as they may have restrictions, such as age limitations.

With a private sale, an independent inspection can be even more important, especially if you do not feel confident checking the car yourself.

VEHICLE HISTORY CHECKS

In addition to having a potential purchase inspected by an independent expert, it is a good idea to conduct a thorough check of the vehicle's history whenever you buy a used car.

With nearly half a million vehicle thefts and the same number of write-offs in the UK every year, it is a wise precaution to have a car checked before buying. This may be slightly awkward as the vendor might be reluctant to let you have the Vehicle Identification Number, but if he or she has nothing to hide, you should be able to persuade them.

Why is it important to perform such a check? It will confirm that the vehicle is not stolen and has not been written off and subsequently repaired. It will show if there is any outstanding finance owing on the vehicle, and will match the vehicle details to the Police National Computer (PNC) and the DVLA records.

Any previous vehicle fraud on your car could result in it being re-possessed. In this case, you will lose all the money you spent on the car.

If the vehicle is stolen and you have paid for it, you will most likely have to give the car back and you will lose your money. Likewise, if the Vehicle Identification Number does not match the registration document, it may be what is known as a 'ringer', where a stolen or repaired car has been given the identity of another car. Again, you will probably lose the car with no recompense.

AUTO ADVICE

Vehicle history checks are a pain, but you will be glad you went to the trouble of conducting one if it turns up a problem.

If the car is recorded as a Category Loss or Total Loss (insurance company terms for written-off cars), it means the car has been accident damaged at some point and had an insurance claim recorded against it. This will reduce its value substantially, and it may mean you cannot subsequently insure it.

History checks can also reveal if a car has been imported, if it has had a registration number change to hide previous accident damage, if it has been accident damaged, and subsequently inspected and approved for use again, or whether it has been recorded as having been scrapped.

Checking the history of a car is easy, as long as you know the registration number and Vehicle Identification Number. Two main bodies offer vehicle information or history checks: HPI and Experian, although these were joined five years ago by Carwatch. Prices for checks can vary, so it is best to shop around. The RAC offers a vehicle history check using HPI, which can be accessed via its website at www.rac.co.uk or 0870 533 3660, as does Infocheck (www.ukcarcheck.com). The AA offers a similar service using information from Experian at www.theaa.com or 0800 085 3007, or you could go direct to HPI at www.hpicheck.com or 01722 422422. The HPI records hold 60 million readings on its national mileage register. If you purchase a history check on-line you will get an immediate report with confirmation and your certificate following within 48 hours.

It pays to get both an independent used car expert check and a full vehicle history report.

The AA and several other organisations offer comprehensive vehicle history checks for a fee.

WHAT HAPPENS IF YOU BUY A STOLEN CAR?

It may be a depressing statistic, but one in eighty cars on the UK's roads is stolen, which means that many people have bought a stolen car and are unaware of its history. Unfortunately, unless they had a vehicle history check carried out, the first they may know of it is when they receive a phone call from the police to tell them their car actually belongs to someone else.

The Office of Fair Trading says that the police can return it to the rightful owner or the insurer, if a claim has been paid out, and despite you buying the car in good faith, you will not be entitled to any compensation. However, if you bought it in good faith, with no knowledge of its history, you are within your rights to refuse to let the police take it from you, unless it is needed as evidence or to establish its identity. If the police do take it, get a written account of their reasons, what they intend to do with the car and when or whether it will be returned to you. You should also write to the police immediately to pursue a title claim.

If a title claim is pending, the innocent buyer is often permitted to continue using the car until a settlement is reached. If the car's identity has been changed, the original details should be reinstated and all records of

history check dos & don'ts

- **DO** remember to go to a reputable company to carry out any vehicle history checks.

- **DON'T** rely on the integrity of the vendor, particularly if it is a private sale and you feel that something is 'not quite right'. When in doubt, have it checked out!

- **DO** shop around the various companies, as prices for history checks can vary.

- **DON'T** try and save money by missing out the history check. The peace of mind you will get from knowing your used car is genuinely legal is well worth the extra money at the outset.

With ever more stringent police monitoring, such as speed checks, stolen cars will increasingly show up on the police database.

tremoved from the Police National Computer. The police or insurance company should next be approached to determine the details of the theft. The car could have been the subject of an insurance fraud and simply disappeared, the owner paid out by the insurance company and the car sold on with a new identity. Until the circumstances are known, the police cannot consider who owns the title to the vehicle, and you are entitled to keep it.

If the original owner made a fraudulent claim, it will be their responsibility to repay the insurance company. You should register the incident with the police as a new crime against you, as the money you paid for the car may have been obtained by deception.

The bottom line is that if you co-operate with the insurance company, you may end up having to pay them some money to keep what you already thought was your car, but at least in many cases you will be able to keep it. However, ensure from the outset that the police have on record that you have no intention of relinquishing your claim to title of the vehicle.

PREVENTION BETTER THAN CURE

It is far better to avoid getting in this predicament in the first place, of course. Other warning signs that the private car you are buying is of dubious heritage are any indications of car dealing when you turn up to view the car, or lots of cars or spare parts around the outside of the vendor's house.

AUTO ADVICE
Always carefully check the windows of a used car. If there are any signs of attempts to remove etched security numbers, walk away.

FINANCE

Cash is always a great persuader when it comes to haggling over the price of a car, but for many people the price of a new or used car is beyond their means, which is where finance comes into play.

The type of finance that you select comes down to personal choice, but shop around for the best deal and check you are quoted the APR, or annual percentage rate, on all loans. The most straightforward form of finance is Hire Purchase. Following a deposit, you will pay monthly payments, but the car remains the property of the finance company until the loan is repaid. As the loan is secured against the vehicle, HP is a

Shop around for your finance in the same way that you would shop around for your car.

finance dos & don'ts

⬥ **DO** remember that with PCPs you do not own the car until the deal is settled, so selling becomes more difficult.

⬥ **DON'T** fall behind on your HP repayments: you could lose your car through a repossession order from the finance company.

⬥ **DON'T** ignore bank or building society loans if you can obtain one. 'Cash-in-hand' gives you room to haggle.

⬥ **DO** make sure you work out the full cost of buying the car and the amount it is likely to be worth once you finally own it. Temptingly low monthly HP repayments can lure you into a long-term arrangement with a high overall cost.

relatively easy form of finance to arrange, but the car can be repossessed at any time. If you sell the car you will obviously still be required to repay the loan.

A personal loan is like HP but it is not secured against the vehicle, so it may be harder to get the loan in the first place.

Finally, there is Personal Contract Purchase, or PCP. At the end you are able to part exchange the vehicle, return it or make a final payment and keep it. This is a convenient method if you plan to change cars regularly.

DEALING WITH SALESMEN

Whether it is a new car or a second-hand car from a dealer that you are interested in, enter the showroom or forecourt with this thought: the listed price is only a starting point for negotiations.

You may not be too comfortable with the thought of having to haggle, but consider that dealers expect to be asked for a discount, and they want your business as much as you want to buy their car.

Do some homework before you go into a showroom. With new cars, better deals can often be found at

Do not be pressurized into accepting a deal on a car until you are completely satisfied with both the vehicle and the finance.

non-franchised dealers or on the internet. Get some quotes beforehand; a salesman may have numerous reasons why buying from him would be better than over the internet or importing, but will struggle to convince you why you shouldn't buy cheaper at another dealership.

The dealer may have special offers or insurance deals, but might then say there are no other discounts available with these. Often the manufacturer

underwrites the special offer, and it does not eat into the dealership's profit at all. Do not accept their excuse that an offer means there is no discount available.

Do not be intimidated by the salesman. They will use a number of sales methods to pressurise you into buying – once you have signed the order form you are legally committed. Similarly with any finance deal. You may be told that you have to sign immediately as the deal will not be offered again. However, take a written copy of the agreement home to think about it if you are not completely happy with the finance package on offer. Do not be pressured into accepting a car that is not what you are looking for. If it is not exactly what you want, walk away or push for more discount. If they say they have to get permission from a manager to offer a discount, ask to speak to the manager who makes the decisions.

Note when a particular model of car is due to be superseded, as dealers will be keen to sell the older model and discounts will be easier to negotiate. Be wary, though, when you are offered a large discount but only a nominal sum for any car you trade in, or a good trade-in price but little or no discount. What you end up paying is the difference between the value of the car you are trading in and the price of the new car, known as the 'cost to change'. This is how much the new car is really going to cost you.

Offering a certain amount of cashback is an incentive many dealers use, but before you sign, check just how long you will have to wait for the cashback. If you are looking for a bargain, see if a dealer has any ex-demonstration cars that have been registered for use for customer test drives. Although not brand new, they will have low mileage. Similarly, some dealerships have cars already registered to themselves, which will be advertised as 'pre-registered' and will be sold at discount prices.

LEGAL PROTECTION

You are protected by law when you buy a car from a dealer, and any second-hand car bought from them has to be of an acceptable standard, bearing in mind its description and price. Any defects should be pointed out by the dealer. Also ask whether there is a pre-sale inspection check list available. If you have any doubts about a vehicle or the integrity of a seller, whether it be a dealer or a private vendor, walk away. There are plenty more cars on the market. It is your money, so you are in charge.

BUYING AT AUCTION

Buying a car at auction can result in purchasing a great bargain, but it can also be a path littered with pitfalls. Here are a few handy tips to arm yourself with before entering a car auction.

Car auction houses range from respected multi-million pound turnover companies, such as ADT Auctions or British Car Auctions, to small town operations frequented by dubious second-hand car dealers looking for new stock. Whichever you choose to go to, go along a few times as a spectator and get a feel for the way the auction house operates. It may help to take a friend along who knows more about cars than you do. Most auction houses run two or more sales each week, and these can take place during the day or in the evening. Visit each sale and you will soon learn which type of vehicle sells best at each sale,

AUTO ADVICE
You can find the address of your local car auction house in Yellow Pages. Check it out thoroughly before you actually bid for a car.

as there will be more traders at the daytime sales and more private buyers and sellers at those held in the evening.

Detailed inspections and test drives are not possible at most auctions, though

Visit the auction house several times as a spectator to get a feel for the way a car auction works before bidding.

Never rush into bidding for a car you are not sure about – there will be plenty of others...

each car has a form attached to the windscreen detailing some history. Many are 'sold as seen', which can reduce any statutory rights you may have should you buy it and it turns out to be faulty. You will be able to make a general inspection of each vehicle if you turn up before the start of the auction.

The beauty of auctions is that the cars come from all areas of the motor trade. What this means is that some reserves are provisional, such as on finance repossessions, and you could end up with a great bargain. Although repossessed cars may have only one key, missing spare wheels or incorrect batteries, most are handed back to the finance company voluntarily and have nothing wrong with them. Main dealers use auction houses to clear their stock of cars taken in part exchange. These can be great bargains as the auction houses usually owe the dealers next to nothing, so will have lower reserves.

Once you have watched the procedure a few times and feel confident, if a vehicle appeals to you it is time to start bidding. Decide how much you want to spend and stick to that limit. Do not be tempted in the heat of the moment to bid above your limit as there will always be more cars at a later date. Listen to the auctioneer when he describes the car, as you may find out details of the car that you had not noticed or could not have known just from a brief inspection.

If you are successful in your bid, you will have to pay in full or pay a deposit with the remainder payable usually within 48 hours. You cannot take the vehicle until the full price has been paid. There is also the auction house's fee, called a Buyer's Premium, which is in addition to the purchase price, the rates of which will be displayed somewhere in the auction hall. Find out how much the fee is likely to be before bidding.

car auction dos & don'ts

▶ **DO** get a feel for the auction house and how it works before you bid. Make sure you know what kind of vehicle it is you want to buy before bidding!

▶ **DON'T** go above your set buying limit.

▶ **DO** make sure you have the funds to pay for what you buy.

SUMMARY

- **Choosing a new car**
  What is your budget?
  What will the car be used for?
  What kind of fuel economy are
  you looking for?
  Insurance group?

- **Choosing a used car**
  Is there a valid warranty?
  What is the mileage?
  Get a history check
  Have it inspected

- **Physical checks**
  Is it comfortable?
  Will your family all fit?
  Is there enough luggage space?
  Test drive it
  Don't view in the rain or dark
  Check for fresh paintwork
  Check exhaust for excessive smoke

- **Get it inspected**
  Shop around for prices
  Is there a warranty?
  What is included?

- **Vehicle history checks**
  Is the car stolen or finance owed?
  Is it registered as written off?
  Shop around for prices

- **Buying a stolen car**
  Don't hand the car to the police
  Report as a crime against yourself
  Pursue title claim to vehicle
  Reinstate vehicle ID
  Clear details from PNC

- **Finance**
  Keep repayments affordable
  Compare APRs
  Shop around for the best deals

- **Buying tips**
  Negotiate or haggle
  Get various quotes
  Don't be intimidated
  Keep 'cost to change' low
  Remain in charge

- **Buying at auction**
  Watch before joining in
  Stick to your limit
  Listen to the auctioneer
  Know what you want

2

Vehicle
Inspect

MOT test cer

te registration mark
cerbyd modur

The legal side of owning a car can seem daunting, but it is actually much simpler than it appears. There are five key things: registration documents for the car; your driving licence; insurance; excise duty (better known as road tax); and the MOT certificate (which is only needed on cars over three years old). You need to have all five to stay legal.

REGISTRATION DOCUMENT

Every car has to have a registration document (V5). This is the car's 'birth certificate', and shows basic information such as make, model, colour and the name and address of the keeper.

At the top of the V5 or V5/C document is the name of the 'keeper'. The keeper is not necessarily the legal owner, but the person who has charge of the car. However, usually the two are one and the same.

When buying a car, you must notify the DVLA (Driver and Vehicle Licensing Agency) using the V5 document. You simply sign it, fill in your name and address, and then

registration dos & don'ts

▸ **DO** keep the registration document in a safe place, but where you can easily get hold of it.

▸ **DON'T** forget to notify the DVLA, using the registration document, if any major adaptations are made to the car.

▸ **DON'T** ever buy a car without a registration document! This will almost certainly mean there is something illegal with the vehicle.

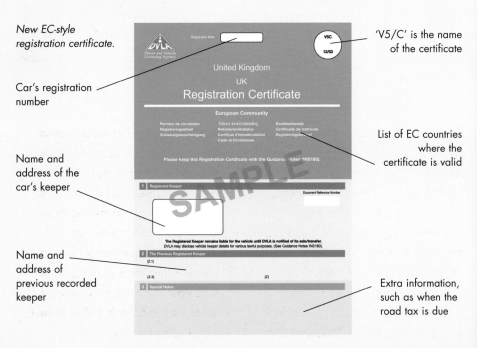

New EC-style registration certificate.

Car's registration number

Name and address of the car's keeper

Name and address of previous recorded keeper

'V5/C' is the name of the certificate

List of EC countries where the certificate is valid

Extra information, such as when the road tax is due

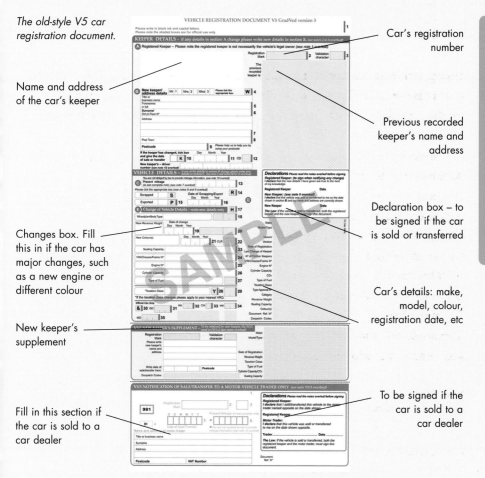

The old-style V5 car registration document.

Name and address of the car's keeper

Car's registration number

Previous recorded keeper's name and address

Declaration box – to be signed if the car is sold or transferred

Changes box. Fill this in if the car has major changes, such as a new engine or different colour

Car's details: make, model, colour, registration date, etc

New keeper's supplement

To be signed if the car is sold to a car dealer

Fill in this section if the car is sold to a car dealer

the previous owner of the car sends it to the DVLA. After a short while, you should receive a new document with your details as the registered keeper. From January 2004, the registration document (V5, above) was gradually replaced by the registration certificate (V5/C, on page 30), which is a European standard.

The DVLA should also be notified (using the registration document) if you make any major modifications to the car, but this only applies to large-scale changes, such as painting the car a different colour, fitting a new engine or a conversion to or from a van (see Chapter 8).

Take care of your car's registration document and keep it in a safe place where you can produce it quickly if called upon, although it should never be kept in the vehicle.

DRIVING LICENCE

You must have a driving licence to drive on public roads. This is proof that you are either learning to drive (a provisional licence) or that you have passed your test (a full licence).

Whether you have a provisional licence or a full one, the licence comes in two parts: the credit card sized photocard and a paper counterpart licence. As well as showing a passport photo of the holder (which has to be renewed every ten years, to keep it up to date), the photocard gives your name, address and driver number (which also cunningly disguises your date of birth). In addition, it also lists the types of vehicle you are permitted to drive. Cars come under Group B, trucks as C, minibuses as D, and so on. Passing the driving test in a car also qualifies you (subject to age restrictions) to drive a tractor or road roller! (You never know when these things might come in handy.)

The paper counterpart licence shows more detailed information,

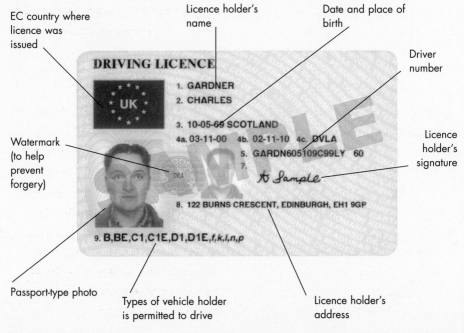

EC country where licence was issued

Licence holder's name

Date and place of birth

Driver number

Watermark (to help prevent forgery)

Licence holder's signature

Passport-type photo

Types of vehicle holder is permitted to drive

Licence holder's address

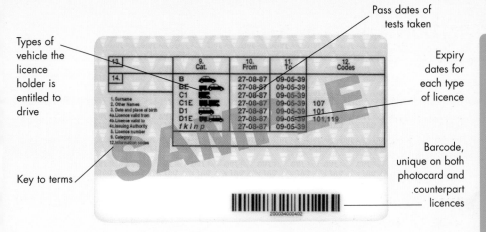

Pass dates of tests taken

Types of vehicle the licence holder is entitled to drive

Expiry dates for each type of licence

Key to terms

Barcode, unique on both photocard and counterpart licences

such as any driving convictions, and acts as a form through which you need to notify the DVLA of any change of address. If you do move house, it is vital that you get your driving licence updated with your new address as soon as possible. Under current legislation, failure to do so could result in a large fine being imposed by the DVLA.

Both provisional and full licences are valid until you are aged 70, but you must tell the DVLA if your health deteriorates in the meantime. The eyesight test, for example, requires

you to be able to read a car numberplate from 20.5m away (20m for cars manufactured from 2001 and later), not just when you take the test, but for as long as you continue driving. So it is up to you to take regular eye tests and ensure you can still pass the 20m test. And if you need glasses or contact lenses to do so, you will have to wear them whenever you drive.

Until you pass the driving test, your licence will be provisional (denoted by the red 'L' for learner in the top left-hand corner of the photocard), so you can only drive with a qualified driver (aged at least 21) in the passenger seat. You will need to display 'L' (for 'learner') plates as well. Once you have passed the test, and have a full licence (shown opposite on page 32), you can tear up the 'L' plates and drive on your own.

AUTO ADVICE
Keep your photocard and counterpart licences together for easy access. You may be asked to produce both.

INTERNATIONAL DRIVING LICENCES

The British driving licence allows you to drive in any EC or EEA country; it is designed to a standard format that will be recognised by the police all over Europe.

However, if you want to venture further afield, you may need to get hold of an International Driving Permit (IDP). The AA, RAC, RSAC and the Green Flag breakdown organisation

licence dos & don'ts

◆ **DO** keep your driving licence safe. You cannot drive legally without it.

◆ **DO** tell the DVLA if you move house, change your name, or if your health deteriorates.

◆ **DON'T** break the law. Six penalty points within two years of passing the test means losing your full licence automatically. You will have to take both theory and practical driving tests again.

◆ **DO** inform the police as soon as possible if your licence is stolen or lost.

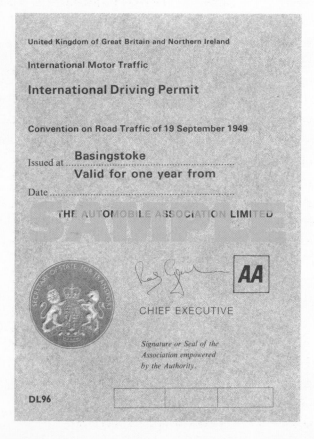

United Kingdom of Great Britain and Northern Ireland

International Motor Traffic

International Driving Permit

Convention on Road Traffic of 19 September 1949

Issued at .... **Basingstoke** ....
Valid for one year from
Date ....

THE AUTOMOBILE ASSOCIATION LIMITED

SAMPLE

CHIEF EXECUTIVE

Signature or Seal of the
Association empowered
by the Authority.

DL96

can advise you whether one is needed for travel to a particular country, and they can also issue IDPs. To apply for one, you must be over 18 and in possession of a full British licence.

AUTO ADVICE
If you need an IDP, you may apply by post to one of the motoring organisations or get one in person from a major post office.

You do not have to be a member of a motoring organisation to apply for an International Driving Permit.

MOTOR INSURANCE

You must be insured to drive on public roads – that is the law. Buying insurance for the first time can be daunting, but there are ways to make the process easier, and less painful on the wallet!

The golden rule for getting insurance is to shop around for the best quote, either through a search on the internet or by ringing around (look up 'Insurance Guide' in the Yellow Pages). There are dozens of insurance companies – some specialize in insuring young drivers, some avoid them – so to save time, a good shortcut is to contact an insurance broker, who will help find you a good deal.

Insurance companies base their premium (the price you pay per year) on a whole range of factors: age and experience of the driver (sadly, young drivers – particularly in years, rather than experience! – are assumed to be a bad risk); the area you live in (there are more accidents and crimes in cities); and, of course, the type of car. The faster, more expensive and flashier the car, the more it will cost to insure. You might have your heart set on a GTi, but insuring it could cost a fortune.

Insurers place cars into one of 20 groups, which give an indication of how expensive they will be to insure. This means that each model of car can be placed in the same group of cars with similar characteristics. There can be a significant spread of groups within a particular model range. As most of the insurer's money will go on repairing cars, the group system is worked out on

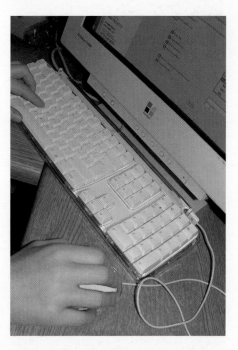

Shop around for the best deal on insurance – the internet is a good place to start.

damage and parts costs, repair times, new car values, security and performance (greater speed and acceleration).

Most family cars will fall into insurance groups 6 to 12, unless they have high powered engines. For example, a Mini is in Group 1, a Ferrari in Group 20, with popular family models such as the Ford Focus, Vauxhall Zafira and Volkswagen Golf slotting in somewhere in between, depending on the engine size and specification of the individual car. All insurance companies use the same system, which makes comparisons easier.

There are three basic levels of car insurance available. Third Party insurance is the legal minimum: if you have an accident – and the responsibility for the accident lies with you – this will cover injury to anyone else or damage to their property.

AUTO ADVICE

Always check the small print for any insurance policy – the cheapest deal is not necessarily the best one.

The next level of cover is Third Party, Fire & Theft: as well as the previous cover, if your own car catches fire or is stolen, the insurance company will pay out. This kind of insurance may not cover theft of radios or items left in the car, so it is worth checking before you buy.

The top level of cover is Fully Comprehensive, which covers any damage to your own car, even if it is your fault. That sounds good, but Comprehensive cover is expensive; if you have a cheap car which is inexpensive to repair, it might simply not be worth it. Ask an insurance broker for advice.

Insurance for young drivers is not cheap, but the longer you drive without having an accident, the larger your no-claims discount will be. This could cut your premium by up to 65% after as little as five years – which is obviously worth staying out of trouble for!

insurance dos & don'ts

- **DO** shop around for the best deal – a little research either over the telephone or on the internet can often save a lot of money.

- **DON'T** ever be tempted to drive without insurance.

- **DO** ask for some insurance quotes before choosing a car – GTi cars can be cheap to buy, but rather expensive to insure...

EXCISE DUTY

Excise duty – better known as road tax – is the amount you pay each year to drive on public roads. It is compulsory, and driving without a valid tax disc could result in a fine of over £1,000.

Road tax is available over 6 or 12 months, and can be renewed at most main Post Offices. The DVLA will send you a renewal form automatically. How much you pay depends on the date of manufacture of your car. Those registered on or after 1 March 2001 will be charged according to their CO_2 emission figure (set for the vehicle's life when new), while those registered prior to that date are charged according to their engine size, from £65 for a small petrol car to £165 for a big diesel.

The road tax disc should be fixed to the bottom left-hand corner of the windscreen (as seen from the driver's seat) on the inside.

Road tax disc.

Serial number of tax disc

Date tax disc expires (30 September 2004 in this case)

Barcode

Amount paid

Make, model and registration number of car

Stamp of issuing authority (usually a Post Office)

SORN

If your car is not being used on the road for some time – for major repairs or because you have decided not to run it for a while – you do not have to pay road tax, but you must make a SORN declaration.

SORN stands for 'Statutory Off Road Notification' and tells the DVLA that your car is not being used on the road. Making a SORN declaration means you do not have to pay road tax, but while it is in force you cannot drive your car on the road or park it on the road. If you do not renew the road tax when it is due, then you must make a SORN declaration instead. Failure to do one or the other will

mean an automatic fine of £80, rising to over £1,000. The DVLA computer records quickly pinpoint who has not renewed their road tax or made a SORN declaration.

When you wish to use the vehicle again, then obtain a new MOT certificate if necessary and buy new road tax.

Tax disc renewal form.

Vehicles kept on private property must all have SORN declarations made.

Keeper's name and address

Car details (make, registration number, etc)

Documents needed to renew tax disc

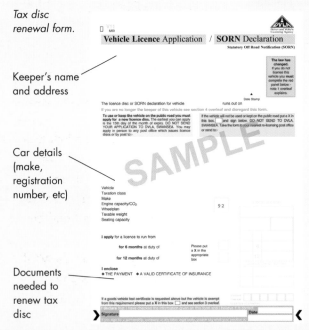

MOT

The MOT is an annual safety test that checks whether your car is safe to use on the road. It covers a whole list of items, as well as the obvious things such as brakes, lights and tyres.

MOT tests are only required for cars over three years old, but they are very comprehensive: lights, steering, suspension, brakes, tyres, seat belts, wipers, horn, exhaust emissions (pollution) and serious rust are all thoroughly checked.

Most garages are qualified to carry out an MOT test (see Chapter 3), and put right anything that needs doing. Many cars fail the

New MOT certificate, effective from 2004.

MOT first time, though the failure is often a simple thing like a blown bulb. All faults, however trivial they seem, must be put right before the car can re-take the test and be used on the road.

When buying a car, a new MOT is a good indication (though no guarantee) that it is in a safe, mechanical condition.

Old MOT certificate, pre-2004.

- **Registration**

  The registration document is your car's 'birth certificate'

  It proves you are the car's keeper

  Keep it in a safe place

- **Alterations**

  Are there any major changes to either the car or your circumstances?

  You must inform the DVLA of any changes so that the registration document can be kept up to date

- **Driving licence**

  The driving licence is your responsibility

  The licence is proof that you are learning to drive or have passed your test

  Keep your licence in a safe place, preferably with you in the car

  It is valid until you are aged 70

  A clean licence means paying less for your insurance

- **Insurance**

  Insurance is compulsory

  Take your time and shop around for the best deal

  Think about the insurance costs when choosing a car – can you afford the insurance for it?

- **Road tax**

  Your car must have road tax to use the roads

  The tax disc can be renewed at main Post Offices

- **SORN**

  Are you taking the car off the road for any reason?

  Have you made a SORN declaration?

- **MOT certificate**

  All cars over three years old must have a valid MOT certificate

  An MOT certificate is simply an indication that a car is safe to use on the roads, but not a guarantee of that

- **The Five Essentials**

  Registration document

  Driving licence

  Insurance

  Road tax

  MOT

3

MOT tests

The MOT test is the British government's way of ensuring that all cars on UK roads are properly roadworthy. Introduced in 1960, this is a compulsory multi-point examination of the key mechanical and electrical parts of any car that is more than three years' old. It offers invaluable peace of mind to all owners of older vehicles.

WHAT IS AN MOT TEST?

If your car is three or more years old, it must be submitted for an MOT test, the purpose of which is to ensure that every vehicle on the road in the UK meets basic roadworthiness standards.

The MOT initials refer to the old Ministry of Transport, the precursor to the current legislative body, the Vehicle and Operator Services Agency (VOSA). Failure to pass an MOT test and attain an MOT certificate means that you will not be able to renew your Vehicle Excise Licence, also known as a tax disc, without which your motor insurance becomes invalid. The MOT test is carried out annually at local testing stations appointed by the VOSA, a government agency. You do not need to be present for an MOT, although testing stations do provide viewing areas for those customers who wish to observe their car undergoing the test.

Various mechanical and structural components are tested, which we will deal with specifically later in this chapter, but there are environmental aspects to the test as well, which ensure that exhaust emissions are kept as low as possible. You are allowed to submit your car for its MOT test up to one month before the existing certificate expires and, on passing, the expiry date of the new certificate will be set one year after that of the existing certificate. This means that if your car fails its test, you will still have one month in order to make the necessary repairs and re-submit it for another test before your current certificate runs out.

SVA TESTS

The SVA (Single Vehicle Approval) testing scheme is a pre-registration inspection for cars and light goods vehicles that have not been type approved to British or European standards. This includes all amateur built and 'personal import' cars, motor caravans and ambulances, Very Low Volume (VLV) Vehicles and any vehicle constructed from donor parts. The purpose of the scheme is to ensure that such vehicles have been designed and constructed to required safety standards before they can be used on the road.

SVA was introduced in 1998 and does not apply to vehicles more than ten years old. If the vehicle is over three years old, a regular MOT test will be required after passing the SVA test.

WHEN AND WHERE ARE MOT TESTS CONDUCTED?

There are approximately 19,000 MOT testing stations in the UK, so there is always one nearby. These are recognised by the MOT sign of three white triangles on a blue background.

Often an MOT testing station will be part of a larger vehicle repair garage. Your local MOT station can be found under 'MOT Testing Stations' in the telephone directory, or by punching 'MOT test' into an internet search engine. Interestingly, one such site – www.ukmot.com – features some pages specifically aimed at women who may feel intimidated by having to visit a garage, offering advice and help, whether they need to go to a garage for an MOT test or general vehicle repairs.

All MOT testing stations are required to comply with mandatory requirements set out by the Vehicle and Operator Services Agency,

Look for the distinctive MOT sign at a garage near you when your car is due for a test.

AUTO ADVICE

If you lose your MOT certificate, you can obtain a copy from the garage that tested your car.

which incorporates its predecessor, the Vehicle Inspectorate. These requirements include the provision of a waiting and observation area, display of the triple triangle sign described above, as well as a 'diesels tested' sign if the station is authorised to test such vehicles, notices detailing testing times, authorised examiners, a Certificate or Authorisation from the VOSA,

SVA testing stations

At the time of writing there are only 22 Single Vehicle Approval test stations in the whole of Great Britain. If you have a vehicle that you think may require an SVA test or wish to obtain an SVA Inspection Manual, contact the Vehicle Inspectorate for details on 020 7944 3000 or via www.detr.gov.uk.

The SVA test is more comprehensive and detailed than an MOT test, and covers different areas. An SVA test is required only once – and only for selected vehicles – prior to registering a vehicle for the first time, most often in the case of an imported vehicle (see page 42).

Garages of all sizes and types will normally conduct MOT tests, but choose a reputable one.

classes tested, test fees and appeals procedure.

Every MOT testing station is required to have a full, up to date, copy of both the MOT Inspection Manual and the Guide to MOT Testing (Fifth Edition). Both of these publications should be made available for viewing on request by a customer. Prices for MOT tests may vary from station to station, though there is an upper price limit set by the VOSA.

UK law states that all cars must undergo an MOT test every year after the third year of registration and that the car be tested on the expiry of the last MOT. Exemptions for driving without an MOT on a public road are outlined on page 51.

The MOT test has been carefully designed and refined over the years to cater for all types of car. The standard multi-point tests are applicable to every registered vehicle, regardless of marque.

The MOT test is designed to ensure a vehicle is mechanically, structurally and environmentally safe to be used on the public road. It should be remembered, however, that an MOT certificate relates only to the condition of those items tested at the time of the test, and not at any later time, and a certificate should not be accepted as evidence of the general condition of a vehicle. The following explains exactly what is tested:

MOT tests are carried out on ramps and rollers so that all parts of the car can be inspected.

Lighting All lighting equipment must be in good condition and fully operational. Bulbs must be working and be of the correct colour. The headlamps must be aimed correctly with no cracked, holed or otherwise broken lenses. The same stipulations apply to all of the following: sidelights; stoplights; indicators; hazard warning lights; fog lights; rear number plate lights; rear reflectors.

Steering The steering rack and joints of your car will be thoroughly checked for play and secure mountings. If fitted, power steering will be checked for correct operation.

Suspension No components must be broken, twisted or bent. All springs must be in good condition. Shock

AUTO ADVICE

See pages 48–50 for simple checks you can make yourself ahead of an MOT test to save time and money.

Brakes are tested by running the wheels in a roller with special test equipment.

absorbers should be free from leaks and operating efficiently. The following will be checked for play: front suspension; front wheel bearings; front wheel drive driveshafts; rear suspension; rear wheel bearings; shock absorbers.

Brakes The hydraulic brake system will be checked for leaks and the mechanical handbrake system (lever and cables) checked for its condition. The performance of the brakes will then be tested by placing the wheels in rollers and activating the test equipment. This will test both the footbrake and handbrake and the brake bias side to side and front to rear. The following equipment will be

checked: handbrake lever and cables; anti-lock brake system; brake pipes and hoses; mechanical components.

Fuel system The fuel tank, pipes and hoses will be checked for leaks and their condition. The fuel cap must seal correctly. Temporary fuel caps are not legal for MOT tests.

Exhaust system The exhaust system will be checked to ensure it is complete and secure with no leaks. Usually at the end of the test a sensor will be inserted in the tailpipe with the engine running to test the level of exhaust emissions.

Tyres and wheels The tyres must be the correct type for the car, of legal tread depth and be in good condition. A spare tyre is not essential for a test, but if fitted must be in a legal state. Road wheels will be checked for condition. The same size wheels must be used at each end of the same axle.

Seats and belts Seats should be secured to the floor of the car and sliding mechanisms should be working correctly. Seatbelts should be secure, functional and in good condition. Inertia reel belts (the type that lock with sudden movement) will have their operation checked.

Windscreen The windscreen must be in good condition with no large cracks. Some small chips are permissible but only in certain areas. The parts swept by the wipers, and in particular the section in front of the driver, will be examined more carefully, and only chips of a certain size will pass the test in these areas (see page 82).

Washers and wipers Washers and wipers must operate correctly. The wipers should not be frayed and must clear the screen sufficiently for a good view through the windscreen.

Horn The horn must be operational.

Mirrors Mirrors on the offside (right) of any vehicle must not be broken or cracked.

Bodywork Front doors must be able to be opened from both the inside and outside of the vehicle, and all doors should latch closed securely. With the car up on a ramp the condition of the underside of the vehicle will be inspected for corrosion in specified areas. It should be noted that the examiner is permitted to use a special small hammer for such an inspection. The exterior bodywork will also be inspected and any jagged edges or serious rust will result in a failure.

Registration plates The condition and security of number plates will be checked, as will the spacing and size of digits.

Vehicle Identification Number This will be checked and recorded on the pass certificate.

PREPARING FOR A TEST

There are some basic checks you can make in preparation for the MOT test, which we will cover on the following pages. Obviously, everything you can do to ensure your vehicle passes the test will increase its chances of doing so.

MOT dos and don'ts

- **DO** make a note of when your vehicle's MOT certificate expires. Forgetfulness is no excuse in the eyes of the law!

- **DON'T** ever drive without a valid MOT certificate, as this invalidates any insurance policy and means that the vehicle is not roadworthy.

- **DO** check the very basics before turning up for the test, such as whether the horn and all lights are working.

- **DO** clean your car thoroughly before your test – dirty light lenses and number plates could result in a failure.

Most motorists dread the MOT test, but it should be looked upon as providing a full safety check on your car by an expert. There are certain basic checks you can carry out yourself, though.

Sitting in the driver's seat, check the windscreen for any cracks or large chips, especially directly in front of the driver. If in doubt, consult an MOT station. It is better to find out now than waste money on a test that will not be passed. Check the horn, wipers and washers, and ensure there is sufficient washer fluid in the reservoir. Ensure the right hand wing or door mirror is clean and not damaged, and seats are securely mounted to the floor.

Check the handbrake. It should not reach its full length of travel, ideally operating fully after three or four clicks of the ratchet mechanism. It should only release when the button is pressed. Make sure that it holds the vehicle stationary on an incline.

Seatbelts should not be frayed, and must be mounted securely. The buckle must also operate correctly. Check both front doors close properly and that they can be opened and shut with interior and external handles.

Moving to the exterior of the vehicle, check that all the lights are working, including the fog lights,

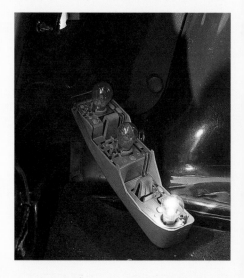

Check all lights are functioning properly and replace any bulbs that are not working.

reversing lights and number plate lights. (The latter is a common cause of failure.) Check the condition of the shock absorbers by pressing down firmly on each corner of the car in turn and letting go. Check that the car rises then settles into its normal position. If the car bounces repeatedly at any corner, the shock absorber is defective and may need replacing.

Check all the tyres, including the spare, to ensure they are above the legal tread depth limit of 1.6mm. Also, check the bodywork for any sharp edges. The tester may feel badly rusted wheel arches are dangerous, but a temporary repair could ensure that the vehicle passes the test. However, such a vehicle is likely to have more rust, and the tester is permitted to use a small hammer (officially known as a 'corrosion assessment tool') to check this. The most likely places are in the sills, which are the lower panels below the doors running between the front and rear wheels, and in the floorpan under the car. Check the sills by using a blunt implement to prod along and under the lower edges. If there is a hole, welding may well be necessary, but at least you will have saved wasting the test fee.

MORE DETAILED CHECKS

The steering can be checked by getting a helper to turn the steering wheel left and right while you listen for any strange noises from the front of the car, and check the wheels turn the moment the steering wheel is turned. Any play here will need rectifying.

If you are mechanically confident, there are other checks you can make. With the car raised off the ground, using a jack and axle stands (never work under a car supported solely on a jack), check the entire exhaust

system for leaks and holes, and repair or replace where necessary.

Check the metal brake pipes and the flexible brake hoses under the car are not corroded, flattened, split or bulging, and that they are attached securely. Check for leaks at all joints in the brake system. Ensure that the handbrake components are not frayed or broken and that the cables are not excessively corroded.

While the car is off the ground, check each of the road wheels in turn for free play in the wheel bearings and ball joints by holding the wheel and shaking it vigorously. If there is any slack, either investigate further or seek professional assistance.

Check the rubber gaiters on each side of the steering rack (on the steering arms attached to an arm on the stub axle assembly) for splits, and ensure any castleated nuts that require locking split pins are so equipped.

The headlamps and other lights must have no cracked, holed or otherwise broken lenses.

Following on from the rudimentary corrosion check above, look out for excessive or severe corrosion of the body structure within 30cm of any point where steering or suspension components attach to the body. Rust holes here can render the vehicle dangerous and unsafe. Suspension struts should also be checked for corrosion and damage, while tyres should be inspected as described on page 68.

Check over the condition of the entire underbody of the car for signs of rust or corrosion in load-bearing areas. These areas can include the chassis, brake master cylinder mounting, steering, seat and seat belt mountings, the sills, cross members and suspension mounts. A common failure is a rusted battery mounting tray, as the battery acid eats into the protective paint, leaving the metal exposed and prone to rust.

Specialist equipment is required to test brakes and emissions, but you can perform some basic checks. With the car off the ground, get someone to press the brake pedal, and try to turn each road wheel by hand. At least you will know whether all the brakes are working! Do likewise with the handbrake.

You can visually check for exhaust smoke. Raise the engine speed to around 2,500rpm for appproximately 20 seconds, return it to idle and observe what comes from the exhaust's tail pipe. Black smoke usually signifies unburnt fuel caused by a dirty air cleaning element or possibly a carburettor or fuel system fault, while blue smoke usually signifies oil being burnt, which means engine wear. Adjustments and tuning can usually reduce the amount of black smoke, but the MOT test is not just a visual check.

With all emissions testing, it is vital that the engine is fully warmed up beforehand. The MOT examiner should do this, but it will help if you drive the car for 20–30 miles if equipped with a catalytic converter, in order to get the best performance from the 'cat'.

Just about the only items that cannot be checked at home are the efficiency of the brakes and the exhaust emissions levels, which both require specialist equipment.

Before the MOT test, fill up the windscreen washer reservoir. If it is empty your car could be failed.

WHAT TO DO IF YOUR CAR FAILS ITS MOT TEST

If your car fails the test you will be issued with a 'failure' sheet, officially called the Notification of Refusal to Issue an MOT Test Certificate (DF). This will list the faults, which will require correction.

Some minor faults entitle you to a free re-test if the vehicle is returned to the garage, with the fault fixed, the following working day, while a free re-test may be offered if the garage is contracted to repair the fault and the vehicle remains on their premises. Many testing stations, however, do offer a free re-test if the car is taken away, repaired and re-presented to them within a certain time frame, usually seven days, when a full inspection is once again carried out.

If your car's MOT certificate has expired and it fails the test, it can only legally be driven on the road when driving from the station where the test took place to a pre-appointed MOT test, or to a garage that will work on the vehicle after an MOT test failure.

These are the only other exemptions: being driven during the test by an authorised person; being towed to be scrapped; being moved under statutory power of removal; being driven after seizure by a customs or police officer; and driving

an imported vehicle from the port of entry to the owner's home. Also, remember that should you drive a vehicle without an MOT certificate at any other time, it will invariably invalidate your motor insurance, as the vehicle will be deemed unroadworthy.

If your car has failed the test, you may wish to appeal against the decision. In such cases, the local VOSA will arrange for an appeal test to be performed, at your expense. If the appeal is upheld, your fee will be refunded. You may also wish to appeal if you think a car has passed a test when it should not have, for instance if you have bought a recently MOT'd car that is subsequently found to be faulty. Known as an inverted appeal, once again the VOSA will arrange an appeal test.

Finally, although some people can become upset when their car fails, perhaps they should be grateful instead, as it could mean a potentially dangerous problem has been spotted.

- **What is an MOT test?**
  Annual roadworthiness test
  Re-test up to one month before expiry
  No MOT, no road tax

- **When and where?**
  Test annually over three years old
  19,000 approved MOT stations in the UK
  Look for the triple triangle sign

- **What is tested?**
  Lights
  Steering
  Suspension
  Brakes
  Fuel system
  Exhaust system
  Tyres and wheels
  Seats and belts
  Windscreen
  Washers and wipers
  Horn
  Mirrors
  Bodywork
  Registration plates
  Vehicle Identification Number

- **Preparing for the test**
  Know when current MOT expires
  Book appointment
  Check lights, horn, washers and wipers
  Arrive early at testing station

- **Basic checks**
  Check windscreen for cracks or chips
  Check mirrors
  Check handbrake
  Check seatbelts
  Check all lights
  Check shock absorbers
  Check tyres for tread depth and width
  Check bodywork for sharp edges
  Visually check exhaust for smoke

- **What if the car fails?**
  Repair faults and apply for re-test
  Many garages offer free re-tests
  Do not continue to use vehicle
  Appeal if justified

4

If just the thought of lifting up your car's bonnet scares you, don't worry – many other drivers feel exactly the same. Although there is no need to take a crash course in mechanics or understand in detail how your car's engine works, by knowing the basics you can allay your fears and prevent or even fix minor problems.

RECOGNISING KEY COMPONENTS AND PARTS

No matter what type of car you have, the key components under most bonnets are nearly always located in similar positions, simplifying recognition should you change vehicles.

UNDER THE BONNET

With front wheel drive cars (where the power from the engine is directed to the front wheels), the engine will almost certainly be mounted transversely across the engine bay. In rear wheel drives (power is directed to the rear wheels) and four wheel drives (power is distributed to all wheels), the engine will be mounted longitudinally, or front to

back in the engine bay. The radiator will be mounted at the front of the car, though an exception is the old style Mini, where it is found at the side of the engine bay.

The brake master cylinder (this takes the force applied to the brake pedal and distributes it evenly to all four brakes) will almost always be

Transverse engine. This type of engine layout is common to front wheel drive cars.

mounted on or near the bulkhead between the engine bay and passenger compartment, and the engine oil will nearly always be added at the top of the engine.

Although the radiator contains the coolant (anti-freeze mixed with water needed to maintain the engine's

key

1. engine oil filler cap
2. engine coolant filler cap
3. brake fluid reservoir
4. windscreen washer reservoir
5. power steering reservoir
6. alternator (only visible on page 54)
7. radiator
8. fusebox and relays (only visible on page 55)
9. engine oil level dipstick
10. air filter
11. battery (only visible on page 54)

operating temperature without overheating or freezing), most cars have an opaque plastic reservoir to allow you to see the level of the coolant and this coolant reservoir may be some distance from the radiator itself. In older cars, the coolant is added directly into the top of the radiator.

Longitudinal engine. You will see this engine layout in rear wheel or four wheel drive cars.

It may sound obvious, but make sure you know on which side of the car the fuel filler cap is located; this will make life easier when refuelling. If your wheels have locking wheelnuts, ensure that you know where the key is in case of punctures, and that it is always kept in the vehicle.

Additionally, make sure that your car has a jack and wheelbrace; a previous owner may have removed them, and if you are stranded at the

AUTO ADVICE

Know the location of the fusebox and all important fluid filler caps on your car. This will help you to avoid costly errors.

roadside with a flat tyre, then that is definitely not the best time to discover they are missing.

If blue smoke is obvious at the exhaust pipe the engine is most likely worn and burning oil. White smoke on start-up is usually not a problem; this often means that there is condensation in the engine which is burning off. Black smoke is a sign of an over-rich fuel/air mixture and may damage catalytic converters. In all cases, these are signs that there is a problem.

1.5 GLSi

proton

key

1. exhaust pipe
2. tyre inflation valve
3. fuel filler cap
4. alloy wheel locknut
5. reverse light
6. indicator light

WARNING SIGNS

Dashboard lights indicate an array of different warnings and faults, depending on the model.

Regular servicing should mean you won't experience problems with the braking system, which is one of the crucial safety elements of any car. Most vehicles have warning lights to alert you to certain faults, such as a faulty handbrake, worn brake pads or low brake fluid level. However, you can pre-empt any faults by noting how the foot brake feels when you push on the brake pedal. If the pedal seems spongy or soft, makes noises or causes the car to pull to one side when in use, consult a mechanic or garage immediately.

The handbrake may also be referred to as the parking or emergency brake and is independent of the main foot braking system. It is most often a hand lever that activates either the front or rear brakes mechanically through a series of cables. These cables can become slack or snap. Even if there are no warning indicators, as a driver you can often tell if the tension feels different when you apply the handbrake. If the amount of travel (leverage) exceeds that specified in your car's handbook, then the handbrake will need adjusting. Do not ignore a handbrake which is obviously loose – it is a very important safety feature on any car.

AUTO ADVICE

It is worth reading your car's handbook in order to familiarise yourself with all the warning lights on your dashboard.

HOW TO TOP UP FLUIDS

There are many engine components that require fluid of one type or another. Over the next few pages, we describe how simple it is to check the fluid levels and top up if necessary.

ENGINE OIL

Oil lubricates the moving parts within an engine, prevents corrosion and helps to keep the engine cool. If the oil level drops too low, an engine will quickly wear internally and serious damage could result.

It is a good idea to check the oil level periodically, especially before a long journey.

Add oil gradually, constantly re-checking the level once it has drained through.

With the engine cold and the vehicle on a level surface, locate the engine oil dipstick [A] and remove it.

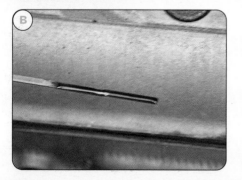

Wipe it clean, replace it and remove it once again, checking that the oil level is between the upper and lower level markings [B]. Add new oil at the filler cap if required (pictured above), wait a minute or so for the new oil to drain to the sump at the bottom of the engine and repeat the procedure with the dipstick until the oil level is at the upper mark.

After time, the oil becomes dirty and loses some of its lubricating ability. While adding fresh oil will help, an oil and filter change is recommended at least every 6,000 miles by most manufacturers.

Fill the coolant reservoir to the 'maximum' level with a water/anti-freeze mix.

COOLANT

The fourth most common cause of breakdowns is overheating, something the coolant is supposed to prevent. Usually the reason for overheating is not the coolant itself, but an associated problem, such as a holed radiator, stuck thermostat, failed water pump, an electric fan that has ceased working or a coolant leak. Occasional topping up with coolant is normal, but if it's a frequent occurrence there is often a leak somewhere. If you cannot spot one at the front of the car, either from the radiator, engine or a hose, check the exhaust. If water persistently drips from the tail pipe, or white smoke doesn't clear, the head gasket may have failed. A trip to a garage will be imminent if this is the case!

As well as preventing the water from freezing in winter, anti-freeze in the coolant helps the engine to run cooler. Check the coolant level frequently, and in winter add the recommended amount of anti-freeze [A]. As with oil, check the coolant level before long journeys. The coolant reservoir [B] will have minimum and maximum levels. Fill the reservoir to the 'maximum' level with the maker's recommended water/anti-freeze mix. If you drive an older car, it may not have a coolant reservoir, in which case the coolant is added directly into the top radiator tank.

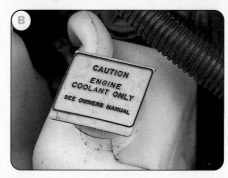

POWER ASSISTED STEERING

Many, though not all, cars have power assisted steering these days. You may not realise there is a problem with this until you hear a hissing noise as you turn the steering wheel or if the steering becomes notchy or juddery. With luck this will just indicate that the power steering fluid level is low. If this is not the case, then the power steering system may be damaged, leading to the steering becoming harder and harder to operate.

Different types of systems use different fluids, though most operate

fluid top-ups dos & don'ts

◆ **DO** check the fluid levels, for every engine system that requires fluid, at least once a month – especially before setting out on a long journey.

◆ **DON'T** check fluid levels when your car is on a slope – you will get a false reading.

◆ **DO** remember to replace the cap every time you fill up or check the levels. You don't want fluid evaporating or leaking out all over the engine.

with automatic transmission fluid. To add fluid to the system or check the level, locate the fluid reservoir [A]. Some will have maximum and minimum level markings on the outside of an opaque reservoir, while others will have a dipstick inside the cap. Some reservoirs are part of the power steering pump, which transfers the fluid to the power steering system components. Add transmission fluid when needed and top up to the correct level [B], taking care not to overfill. This varies depending on the particular model, so follow the instructions given in the car's manual.

More new cars now have electric power assisted steering (EPAS) systems, which use an electric motor to provide additional directional control. The EPAS system is gradually replacing the hydraulic steering system, as EPAS does not require engine power in order to operate.

BRAKE FLUID AND CLUTCH FLUID

The brakes are probably the most important components of a vehicle, but they won't work without brake fluid. As the brake pads wear down the fluid level drops accordingly, but needing to regularly top up will indicate a leak somewhere. For example, if brake slave cylinders within the brake drum leak badly, you'll notice brake fluid seeping from the bottom of the drum on the inside of the wheel. Brake pipes themselves can also leak fluid, or the brake master cylinder can leak either externally or, more difficult to spot, internally.

The brake fluid reservoir is most often found on the master cylinder, which is almost always mounted on the bulkhead between the engine and passenger compartments. Topping up the fluid is simply a matter of locating the reservoir [A], removing the cap so as not to spill any fluid, and adding fluid [B] to the

AUTO ADVICE

Brake fluid is poisonous and corrosive to paint. Remove drips from skin or paintwork with plenty of water immediately.

specified level, usually marked on the outside of the opaque reservoir [C].

Some cars have hydraulically operated clutches (your handbook will tell you if this is the case). If so, the clutch fluid reservoir will probably be located alongside the brake fluid reservoir. Locate and fill as necessary.

MANUAL AND AUTO TRANSMISSIONS

The transmission of a vehicle, commonly referred to as a gearbox, is used to select a gear to suit engine speed either manually or automatically.

Whatever type of transmission your car has, it needs lubrication. In the case of an automatic, transmission fluid is a necessary part of the transmission's function, so needs regular checking. Consult your car's handbook for the exact location of the gearbox filler plug, as well as the type of transmission fluid to use.

To check the automatic transmission fluid level, the engine should first be warm, preferably after a short drive to pump fluid through the transmission. With the engine running and the gear selector in 'park' or 'P', locate the

transmission fluid

▶ Always check your handbook to ensure you use the correct transmission fluid, as several types are available.

▶ Manual gearbox oil is not the same as engine oil. Use only the type specified for your vehicle.

▶ Ensure the vehicle is on level ground before checking the transmission fluid or oil level.

▶ Some vehicles are equipped with gearboxes which are sealed, in which case the transmission fluid does not need checking.

dipstick tube [A] and remove the dipstick. As with the engine oil dipstick, markings will indicate the upper and lower limits of fluid level [B]. Wipe clean and replace before removing again to check the level.

If topping up is required, most automatic transmission fluids are sold in bottles with plastic tubes extending from their caps, which makes filling through the dipstick tube easy. Recheck the level after topping up.

If your car has a manual gearbox, checking the oil will invariably mean accessing the underside of the car, which may be better left to a garage.

The jets can usually be cleared by inserting a pin into the nozzle [C]. Occasionally, in severe winters, the washer jets may freeze and it may take a while for the engine heat to thaw them. Avoid continually pressing the washer switch as you could damage the pump motor.

WINDSCREEN AND HEADLAMP WASHERS

You won't appreciate how important windscreen washers are until you have a dirty windscreen. Remember, too, that your headlights will be just as dirty, cutting down on their effectiveness at night. Not all cars have headlamp washers, but if yours has, check and top up the fluid regularly with the specially formulated screenwash available for windscreen washers, which also prevents it from freezing in winter.

Locate the windscreen wash reservoir under the bonnet of your car [A], remove the cap and fill to the required level [B] with screenwash. Remember to top up the reservoir for any rear screen washer your vehicle may be fitted with. This is often located in the boot, but refer to your manual.

If the reservoir is full and the washers still don't appear to work, you may have a blocked washer jet.

WASHER FLUID ONLY

TOPPING UP THE BATTERY

Car batteries come in various sizes and power outputs. A bigger engine will require a battery with a higher power output capacity. Modern cars are designed to take a specific sized battery for each model. There are also various types of battery, with most modern versions being maintenance free – a fit-and-forget-about-it battery!

Conventional batteries, however, require periodical checking to ensure the electrolyte – the fluid inside the battery – is at the specified level. These batteries have plastic plugs on their top surface, which are then removed to enable you to check the fluid level. Some of these plugs screw on, some twist on and some have to be prised off with a screwdriver or similar implement. It will be obvious to you which type is fitted when you come to remove them.

Remove all the plugs [A] and visually check that the metal plates inside each cell are submerged in fluid. Some batteries have a level gauge inside the cell to help with this. If any cell is running low of fluid, top up with distilled water [B], which is available at any motor spares shop or garage. In emergencies, cold water from a boiled kettle will suffice.

Replace the plugs securely. If your battery is flat it will still require charging (see page 67), but topping up the fluid will ensure that it can now operate at full working capacity once it has been recharged.

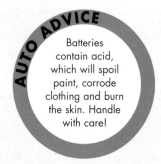

AUTO ADVICE

Batteries contain acid, which will spoil paint, corrode clothing and burn the skin. Handle with care!

HOW TO DISCONNECT AND REMOVE THE BATTERY

If you need to replace the battery or connect it to a battery charger outside the car (for example, for overnight charging), then it will have to be removed from the vehicle.

Why would you want to replace a battery? Well, the battery powers not just the ignition and lights, but also supplies the power for the heater fan, heated rear window, stereo, fuel injection and other computer controlled functions of a modern car. If the battery is not up to par, the first you will become aware of it is when the starter becomes sluggish or refuses to operate altogether.

Removing the battery may be a

Continual short journeys, often with the headlights on, have weakened this battery.

> ### battery dos & don'ts
>
> **DO** keep your battery clean, fully topped up with ionized (distilled) water and properly charged.
>
> **DON'T** ever put water straight from the tap into your battery – it will destroy it.
>
> **DO** replace your battery on a regular basis. Your car will thank you for it!

problem if your car is fitted with an alarm, and especially if it has a coded stereo unit, which will disarm itself once the battery is removed. This is not a problem if you know the code, but there are many second-hand cars where the code is not known. If you are at all unsure, have your battery replaced by one of the many battery/tyre/exhaust specialists. They can plug a neat little gizmo into your car's cigarette lighter to maintain a power supply to the stereo and alarm while the car battery is disconnected.

Remove the negative (black) terminal first using a spanner to undo the securing nut, then the positive (red lead) [A], to avoid causing any sparks. With the battery disconnected, the clamp which holds it in place can be undone [B]. Quite often these can be corroded and may need oiling before attempting to undo the nut. Different cars employ various methods of clamping down the battery, such as fitting over the battery or clamping the lower lip of the battery to the battery tray, as shown here.

With the battery clamp undone, lift the battery from the car and check the battery tray for corrosion. You do not want your new battery falling out of the engine bay! Make sure your new battery has the same type of terminals

as your old one. There are square terminals, which the leads bolt to, and round 'post' type terminals, which the leads clamp onto. Check, as well, that the positive and negative terminals are in the same position. The leads are connected to the new battery (positive first, then the negative) before the battery clamp is tightened. Add some form of terminal protector to prevent corrosion [C]. This can be bought from accessory shops, but petroleum jelly works just as well. Without protection the terminals, especially the positive one, will corrode and become difficult to remove in future.

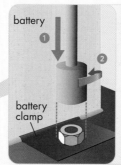

battery

battery clamp

To remove the battery clamp from the battery tray, carefully place the socket over the nut [1], then twist until loose [2]. The nut may need lubricating if there is any visible corrosion.

You should not need to charge your car's battery using a battery charger unless it has gone flat. Common reasons for this will be that the car has been left for some time or the alternator, which usually charges the battery, is not working. Similarly, if you leave your headlights on with the engine turned off, the battery may drain and go flat.

It is possible to 'jump start' the car using jump leads and another vehicle. This will not recharge your battery, but once started, and providing you travel a sufficient distance, the alternator will recharge the battery. Details on how to use jump leads are on page 98.

You can charge a battery using a charger in situ or out of the vehicle (for example, overnight). Whichever method, the battery leads must be disconnected before connecting the charger, which means the points about alarms and stereo equipment on page 65 will be relevant. Some

Connect the red positive charger lead to the positive battery terminal and the black negative lead to the negative battery terminal. Finally, connect the charger to a mains supply and switch on.

chargers can be set to fast charge or 'trickle' charge for a slow charge over long periods, while others, usually cheaper models, are only set to trickle charge. It is usually better to trickle charge but depends how quickly you need the battery up and running.

Connect the red positive charger lead to the positive battery terminal and the black negative lead to the negative terminal. Adjust the charging rate if necessary and connect the charger to a mains supply. When charged, disconnect the supply before removing the leads from the battery.

AUTO ADVICE

When using a battery charger with the battery still in the car, disconnect your battery's leads before charging.

Tyres are your only point of contact with the road surface, so it makes sense to look after them and monitor their condition. In addition to each tyre being inflated to the correct pressure, the condition and depth of the tread is equally important.

The minimum legal tread depth in the UK is 1.6mm, which can be measured using a tread depth gauge. Penalties for using tyres below the legal limit can be severe, including driving licence endorsements and large fines. Badly worn tyres and those in poor condition with cuts and bulges in the sidewalls are also more susceptible to punctures and catastrophic failure. Check the condition of your tyres regularly, particularly for low tread, worn areas or any bulging.

A tread depth gauge can measure whether tyres comply with the legal tread depth.

All tyres will wear eventually, but you may notice the tyres on your car wearing unevenly. For instance, they may wear on the outside edge only, the inside edge or, less commonly, in the centre, while the rest of the tread is fine. Wearing on either edge could be caused by wheel misalignment, which can be checked at a tyre dealership, a process known as 'tracking'. More seriously, the same type of wear could also be caused by worn or modified suspension.

Wear on both the inside and

Badly worn tyres are dangerous and liable to severe penalties and fines.

This photograph shows a tyre that is worn mostly on the outside edge.

worn outside edge

tyre dos & don'ts

▶ **DO** replace the valve every time you change a tyre. By doing so, you guarantee airtightness and extend the life of your tyres; valves deteriorate under the action of centrifugal force.

▶ **DO** check the balancing. As well as suppressing vibrations, this will help avoid premature wear, not only on tyres but also on the suspension and wheel bearings.

outside edges of a tyre can occur when a tyre is under-inflated; a tyre that wears in the centre of the tread can be attributed to over-inflation, which we will cover on page 70.

TYPES OF TYRE

Modern cars are fitted with radial ply tyres, but older vehicles were equipped with crossply tyres. These two types of tyre offer different handling characteristics. The only time mixing the two types is legal is when radials are fitted on the rear and crossplies on the front of a vehicle. If replacing tyres, opt for radials, and preferably keep to the same make and tread pattern.

IDENTIFYING TYRES

All tyres have markings on the sidewall to identify the size and speed rating. Below is a radial ply tyre bearing the following mark: 215/65 R 15 102H.

The 215 denotes the tyre width in mm; 65 is the tyre height to width as a percentage. The R denotes that the tyre is radial ply construction; 15 is the wheel diameter in inches; 102 is the maximum load rating that the tyre is capable of carrying at its maximum recommended speed; and H is the speed rating for that maximum speed, in this case up to 130mph.

The marking on this sidewall denotes the size and speed rating of the tyre.

It is important to maintain the correct tyre pressure for your vehicle, as not only will the tyres wear more rapidly if not inflated correctly, but the handling of the vehicle will suffer. For example, if the pressure in one tyre is particularly low, you may notice the car will seem to pull slightly to one side. In addition, lower than recommended pressure in the tyres will cause more drag when driving, resulting in a loss of fuel economy.

Tyre pressures should be checked regularly to maintain your vehicle's optimum performance and roadholding. Remember to check the spare tyre, too, as, should you ever need to fit it, the last thing you want is to discover it is flat!

Tyre pressure can be checked at most petrol stations, which will have compressed air available to inflate

Digital gauges generally give the most accurate tyre pressure readings.

tyre pressure dos & don'ts

DO check your tyre pressures every two weeks or at least once a month, as this will ensure your vehicle maintains its best roadhandling capability.

DON'T ever over-inflate your tyres, as the vehicle's roadhandling will suffer and the tyre treads will wear in the centre.

DO bear in mind that tyre pressures should be checked 'cold' – that is, before you have driven very far.

Manual pressure gauges are useful for checking tyres at home.

the tyres. Most are free to use, although some may require tokens from the forecourt attendant. Remove the cap from the valve and push the end of the airline onto the valve stem, locking it into place. A gauge either on the airline or on the pump housing will show the pressure in the tyre. Inflate the tyre until it reaches the recommended pressure, shown in your handbook or sometimes on a chart next to the air pump. Manual and digital pressure gauges are also available to enable you to check tyre pressure at home.

A variety of pumps can be bought to inflate tyres from home. Electric pumps are the most expensive of these and can be plugged either into your car's cigarette lighter socket or into the mains electricity, depending on the model. While the dearest of the group, electric pumps require the least effort on the part of the user. Manual pumps come in both single and double cylinder form, with the double version inflating the tyre more quickly.

(usually a clip) and press down on the lever with your foot.

The gauge on a footpump usually has two needles. Set the red indicator to the manufacturer's recommended pressure. The black needle will rise up the scale; when it reaches the same point as the red needle, the desired pressure will have been reached.

When connecting the hose to a valve, push the hose onto the valve as far as possible [1], then release the lock mechanism [2] on the pump's hose, so that the connection made is a tight fit.

MANUAL PUMP

To operate a manual pump, remove the cap from the tyre valve and attach the airline as described previously. In some cases, a hubcap or wheel trim may need to be removed to access the valve. Attach the end of the pump's tube to the valve, release the lock mechanism on the pump

Press up and down with your foot until the gauge shows the correct pressure reading.

REPLACING WINDSCREEN WIPER BLADES

As well as being unable to clear a windscreen properly, faulty wiper blades are illegal. They wear and split, and should be checked regularly, and preferably replaced annually.

In extreme cases, if the rubber blade on a windscreen wiper splits badly enough, the metal part of the blade could scratch the glass. Replacement blades are inexpensive, yet can make a vast improvement and help you see more clearly through the windscreen.

To check your blades, carefully lift the wiper arm away from the windscreen and check for splits or tears in the rubber (below). If they are damaged or do not wipe the glass very well, they should be renewed. Lay the wiper arm back on the glass. If it appears that the blade is not pushing hard enough onto the windscreen, it may be that the springs in the wiper arms themselves have weakened. This

Split wiper blades will severely hinder your vision and could cause you to have an accident.

windscreen wiper dos & don'ts

- **DO** check the condition of your wiper blades on a regular basis.

- **DON'T** use your wipers on a dry screen, as this will wear them out quickly, causing them to split.

- **DO** remember to replace your blades annually as a matter of course.

- **DON'T** forget to release frozen wipers before switching on. You could damage the wiper motor if they remain stuck!

will mean new arms – although this usually only occurs on older cars.

Replacement wiper blades are available at motor accessory shops and main dealers specialising in your make of car. Manufacturers use different types of fitment adaptor to connect the wiper blade to the arm, and different models use blades of different lengths. To ensure you buy the correct blade to fit, you will need to know the make, model and year of manufacture for your car.

To fit new blades, lift the wiper arm away from the windscreen. Most will reach a position where they 'lock' and stay upright, but if yours is not this type, take care not to let it spring back and possibly break the windscreen as you remove the blade.

To remove the blade from the arm, turn it at 90 degrees to the arm, depress any securing tabs and slide

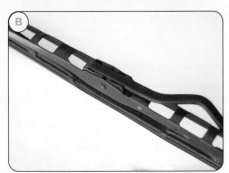

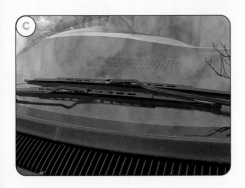

the blade and plastic adaptor from the wiper arm [A]. As mentioned there are several types of adaptor. These generally slide and clip into place, but refer to the handbook for your specific make and model of car if the securing method is not obvious.

If you have bought your new wiper blades from a motor spares or accessory shop, you may find that they are supplied with a selection of different adaptors. These are normally number-coded to specific models of cars – full details are usually given on the box. Select an adaptor that matches those on the original blades and fit to the new blade, usually by sliding and pressing the part into place [B]. Reverse the removal procedure and fit the new wiper blade to the arm, ensuring that it clicks firmly into place before carefully lowering the arm and placing the new blade on the screen [C]. Wet the screen and check the new wiper blades work properly before using the car.

Take care of your new wipers by cleaning the blades occasionally and washing your car regularly. In winter, when ice may form on the windscreen, carefully free the wiper blades before turning them on, as they may be frozen to the screen. Failing to do this could cause them to tear or split, or even worse, damage the wiper motor.

CHECKING THE LIGHTING SYSTEM

How often do you see a car on the road with one or more lights not working? It should be obvious to a driver when a headlight is not working, but the rear, brake and side lights can go undetected for a while as the driver cannot see them while driving.

On many vehicles it is relatively easy to tell when an indicator stops working, as the indicator lamp on the dashboard will flash more quickly. This is not always the case, so it is good to periodically check the lights around the exterior of your vehicle.

With the ignition key turned to the first position, that is where the electrical systems operate but the engine is not on, turn on the sidelights and check around the car, front and rear, to see if they are lit. Repeat for the fog lamp if fitted. Select reverse gear with the engine off and the handbrake on, to check the reversing lamp or lamps.

Switch on the hazard warning lights to check they flash. The hazard warning lights work independently from the indicators, so it is important to check both. For the brake lights, sit in the car and press the brake pedal, still with the ignition switched to the first position, and a friend outside the car. If there is no-one available, try using a reflection in a house or shop window to see the lights.

Headlight alignment can be checked by aiming dipped beams at a wall or garage door.

Next, check the headlights, both dipped and main beam. It is important also that the headlight beam is correctly adjusted for each light. A rough gauge of alignment can be made by turning the dipped beams on with the vehicle roughly 3m from a wall or garage door, and checking both headlamp beams are at the same level. Should either beam be mis-aligned, consult your handbook to adjust.

Check the condition of the headlight lenses. A holed lens will probably result in an MOT test failure. On some vehicles the lens can be changed but a new headlight unit may be required.

REPLACING A HEADLIGHT AND SIDELIGHT BULB

Knowing how to change a headlight or sidelight bulb will save you on garage bills. When travelling in Europe, it is also a requirement to carry a spare set of bulbs, so also being able to fit them makes sense!

With most modern cars, the bulb is accessed from the rear of the headlight, which you get at from inside the engine bay. Cars such as old style Minis require the headlight unit to be removed from the front to access the bulb, but this is rare nowadays. Even with this type of lamp, the bulb still mounts from the rear of the lamp unit, but the lamp has to be removed from the car first.

Obviously there will be variations between different makes of car. Some will have covers over the rear of the headlights which will need to be removed, or the battery will require removal for access on others (see

bulb changing dos & don'ts

▸ **DO** make sure the lights are switched off before replacing bulbs.

▸ **DON'T** ever handle the glass on new halogen headlamp bulbs.

▸ **DO** take the old bulb with you when buying a replacement, to make sure you purchase the same type.

page 65), but the bulb holder itself will look similar to that shown [A]. The headlight wiring is the three-sided connector plug in the centre of the rear of the lamp unit with three wires leading from it. The smaller connector with two wires is the sidelight wiring.

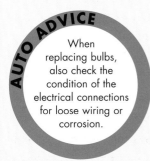

AUTO ADVICE

When replacing bulbs, also check the condition of the electrical connections for loose wiring or corrosion.

headlamp wiring

sidelight wiring

To change a sidelight bulb, simply twist and remove this connector, complete with the bulb holder and replace the bulb (sidelight bulbs are almost always of the push-in type). Finally, twist the connector with the new bulb back into place.

To replace the headlight bulb, firstly remove the wiring plug from behind the bulb by twisting and pulling, then the rubber seal through which the electrical bulb connectors pass [B]. This will reveal the bulb itself and the clip which holds it in place [C]. Carefully release the sprung clip, fold it out of the way, and remove the blown bulb [D]. Most bulbs today are the halogen type (as shown).

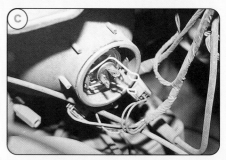

You may find that the glass bulb is spherical; however, the replacement procedure is the same for both types. Halogen bulbs have projections in three positions around their edge, and so can only be fitted in one position. Be careful not to touch the glass bulb on halogen types with your fingers, as this will drastically reduce the life span of the bulb. Always handle bulbs by holding on to the electrical connectors. Once you have replaced the bulb, simply reverse the removal procedure.

Lights also may not work if a fuse has blown (see box, right). Fuses protect components from damage and possible fire, like fuses in your home.

fuses

Fuses are designed to break when an electrical circuit becomes overloaded. Having changed a bulb, if it still doesn't work, then check the fuses. The location of the fuses in your car, as well as the amp rating required for a fuse in each particular application, will be detailed in your manual. Remove the old one by gently pulling and replace with a new one. If it is still not solved, have the problem checked.

REPLACING AN INDICATOR/ BRAKE LIGHT BULB

As with the procedure to replace a headlight bulb, various car manufacturers employ different ways of mounting tail light assemblies and accessing them.

To access the rear of a tail light assembly, you may have to remove parts of the interior trim, although there are usually access doors in the trim panels, which just unclip. Once accessed, the lamp assembly and bulb holder will look similar to the one shown [A]. In this instance, the lamp assembly bolts to the bodywork with four nuts. The bulb holder is attached to it using a couple of clips located in the recesses in the white housing. Release these clips to remove the bulb holder from the lamp unit [B]. In the case of a smashed light lens, the lamp assembly can now be unbolted from the car and replaced.

It should be obvious which bulb has blown, as it will most likely be blackened inside. If you are unsure, hold the bulb holder in one hand, look at the lens on the outside of the car and select the bulb which corresponds to the section of the lens that was not working. Remove the bulb by pushing it into the holder slightly and twisting anticlockwise [C].

The blown bulb (right) will normally be blackened inside.

Replace the bulb and reverse the removal procedure. Some bulbs have a double element in them for combined rear and brake light applications (known as a bayonet fitting, with offset securing pins for correct fitment), while others will have single elements (indicators, and applications where the brake and tail lights are separate). Ensure you use the correct bulb, which will be obvious from the bulb holder.

With the bulb changed, check that it is working properly before the bulb holder is replaced in the lamp assembly. On some cars, however, this is not possible as the bulb holder is not earthed until it is replaced. Always check, though, as it may not have been the bulb that was at fault, but some form of wiring problem.

REPLACING SIDE REPEATER LAMP BULBS

Side repeater lamps are standard equipment nowadays and are easily overlooked when it comes to checking the operation of lamps. They are simple to replace, although there are a number of ways in which the light unit itself is mounted. Some just need pushing either backwards or forwards to release the unit from the bodywork, others require twisting until they release, while some [A] require a blunt instrument to be inserted in a slot at one end to release a sprung clip.

With the lamp unit released, twist the bulb holder from its position to enable the bulb to be replaced [B].

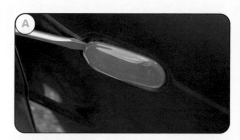

REPLACING A BROKEN DOOR MIRROR

As discussed in Chapter 3, a damaged driver's door mirror will cause your car to fail its MOT test, although you really should replace any broken mirror as a matter of course.

If it is only the mirror glass that is damaged [A], you will most likely be able to source a suitable replacement from a motor parts or accessory shop. Such replacements are self-adhesive [B] and can be stuck over your damaged mirror once the existing glass has been thoroughly cleaned. However, if the glass is too badly damaged or missing, you will have to carefully remove it all, including any old adhesive, before fitting the new glass. Whichever way the new glass is fitted, ensure it is correctly aligned in the casing before final fitment.

If you cannot find a self-adhesive replacement or your glass is missing you will need a replacement sourced from a main dealer specializing in your make of car. Most clip into place, but seek advice on the exact method if you are unsure, and take care not to break the new mirror during fitment.

If the mirror casing is damaged or you have special heated glass, you will have to buy a replacement from the manufacturer of your car, as you cannot simply place the new mirror on top. Mirror casings are mounted from inside the vehicle, through the door structure, and to access this usually requires removing the interior door trim. You may wish to have such parts professionally fitted.

FITTING A NEW PETROL CAP

You may need to fit a new cap if your old one's locking mechanism has seized, or you have forgotten to replace it at the filling station, or you just want a different style filler cap.

Caps with keys can be locked in several ways.

The aircraft style filler cap is a popular choice.

If you have lost the key or the lock has seized while the cap is on the car, you will obviously need to remove it before you can fit another. If you are replacing the cap with another standard one, and buying it from your local main dealer, there is a good chance they will be able to undo the old lock. But if they are unable to, or you are desperately in need of fuel, take the car to a local garage or even a locksmith. You may not be able to use the cap afterwards, though.

Temporary fuel caps are available at most garages and accessory shops, although it should

Temporary fuel caps are useful as a stop-gap measure.

be stressed that is all they are intended for – temporary use. These 'push-in' caps, while capable of stopping fuel spillage, allow fuel fumes to escape easily, so you should buy a proper replacement as soon as possible.

When fitting the new cap, determine which type it is. Some are turned clockwise then the key turned to lock them, some turn clockwise until a 'click' is heard, and the key only used to unlock the cap, and others have no lock as they are mounted behind lockable flaps or doors that are part of the car bodywork.

FREEING FROZEN AND RUSTED DOOR LOCKS

Motoring in the winter brings with it many hazards, such as icy roads. But you have to first get into your car, and if it is kept outside you may find your door locks frozen and inoperable!

You may be lucky enough to have a heated key, but if not, other means of thawing the lock will be required. A hairdrier can be used [A] if you have a power supply close to hand, while hot water from a recently boiled kettle may also work, though this can make matters worse if it freezes again. Use as a last resort. Carefully warming the key over a gas ring on a cooker is probably the easiest way.

If the temperature is particularly cold and the door rubbers on your vehicle are exceptionally good, you may find the rubbers freeze to the door frame, and the door is impossible to open. In this instance, you may have to break out the hairdryer or kettle and apply heat around the rear and upper door shuts.

You may find your door locks become stiff or seize up altogether. If this happens, liberally spray the lock barrel with a proprietary penetrating fluid [B]. Insert the small plastic tube in the nozzle and place directly into the lock barrel. Then insert the key and

spend a few minutes operating the lock from side to side. Apply more oil and repeat until the lock frees up.

Clearing the screen with boiling water is not recommended, as the hot water on the cold glass can cause the screen to crack. Keep an ice scraper handy and spend a few minutes clearing all the windows or invest in a de-icer spray for such occasions.

REPAIRING WINDSCREEN CHIPS AND SCRATCHES

A damaged windscreen, whether it be chipped or scratched, will impair the driver's vision of the road, and will most likely damage the windscreen wipers, leading to further restricted vision.

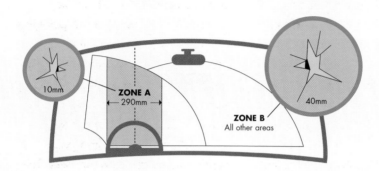

This illustration shows the extent of windscreen damage that is permissible in an MOT test.

Your screen may only be scratched, in which case you may be able to polish the scratch away with glass polish or jeweller's compound. Do not use any polish or compound for bodywork, as it may damage the glass further.

The MOT test includes the condition of the windscreen, and contains limits relating to permissible damage. Most important is the area directly in front of the driver, zone A in the diagram. In this area, any chips or cracks must be no larger than 10mm in diameter or length. Damage to any other part of the screen must be no more than 40mm in diameter or length.

A damaged screen does not necessarily mean it has to be replaced, as many chips and cracks can be repaired. Many windscreen replacement companies offer repair services, limited by the size of the chip and which part of the glass is affected. Repairs can only be effected to the outer layer of a laminated windscreen, and should be carried out as soon as possible after the damage occurs, as cracks can spread and chips may fill with dirt and moisture.

After cleaning the damaged area, a vacuum is formed over it and resin used to fill the chip or crack. Ultraviolet light is then used to cure the resin, leaving the damage almost invisible, and saving the time and expense of replacing the windscreen.

REPAIRING BODYWORK DAMAGE

All cars pick up small knocks and scratches, often due to adjacent car doors opened without care in car parks. Most, including small dents, can be removed without resorting to repainting.

When you scuff your car against another, or against a post or bollard, it will leave traces of the paint from the offending item on your car's paintwork. This can usually be removed using a colour restorer, which is a very fine abrasive, and is often used to restore the shine on an older car on which the paint has lost its shine and faded. The way a colour restorer works is by removing a layer of paint, so it is ideally suited to removing any paint that should not be on the car!

Use a soft cotton cloth or mutton cloth, available at accessory shops in rolls, to apply the colour restorer liquid in a circular motion [A]. Take care not to rub too hard on the area surrounding the scuffed paint, as there is a danger you could rub through the paint. Be especially careful with metallic paint. This is applied in two stages, the base coat of colour then a clear lacquer coat on top. You will not notice the clear layer coming off on your cloth and may rub through to the base coat, leaving the area looking

dull or satin in finish without the lacquer. When the offending paint has been removed, use a clean cloth to remove the excess colour restorer [B]. If the paint is proving difficult to shift, you could use a fine rubbing compound, available from motor spares shops or automotive paint suppliers such as Brown Brothers. This is coarser than the colour restorer, but

advice

- When using either colour restorer liquid or rubbing compound, take care not to rub too hard, particularly at the outset, and be especially careful when you are applying it to metallic paint.

- If you need to use touch-up aerosol paint or a stick, you must have the exact colour code match for your car.

does, however, remove existing paint even faster, so take care.

SCRATCHES

If you have scratched your car's paintwork, you may find rubbing compound will remove the scratch if it has not broken through the paint to the undercoat, or on metallic cars through the clear lacquer to the coloured basecoat. If this is the case, use the rubbing compound followed by polish to restore the shine to the paintwork.

If a scratch has broken through the paint, it will need touching up. Aerosol cans of touch-up paint are available from accessory shops for most modern car colours, but are not required for touching in scratches, where a touch-up stick will suffice. This is a small container of paint with a brush built into the lid. After cleaning the area surrounding the scratch, use

colour restorer or compound lightly to prepare the area. Though this step is not essential it will ensure a better colour match once the paint has been applied. After mixing the paint by shaking the container, use the brush to apply the paint, brushing along the scratch, not across it, in an attempt to fill the groove. Do not let the paint build up above the original surface, and with a metallic car, leave the colour coat slightly below the surface as you will need to add a clear coat too. Wait at least overnight, preferably longer, for the paint to dry, without letting it get wet in the meantime.

Next, use the rubbing compound, polishing along the scratch then over the scratch

AUTO ADVICE
Take care not to rub through paint with compound. Always match the paint code to the touch-up stick.

and surrounding area in a circular motion, to blend the new paint with the original. Stonechips can be treated in the same way as scratches.

Before you buy a touch-up stick you will need to know the paint code for your car to buy matching paint. The paint code will be found on the Vehicle Identification Number (VIN) plate under the bonnet. This is usually located on the slam panel where the bonnet catch is situated or on one of the inner wings. If you are not sure, either call your local dealer to find out or take the vehicle along when you buy the paint.

DENTS

Small dents on a car's bodywork are again often caused in car parks, when one door bangs against another. Most such dents can be removed without a trip to a body and paint shop, as there are numerous companies nationwide that specialise in paintless dent removal. Many companies deal extensively with the motor trade, such as the operative pictured on the right working on sales cars at a dealership, but will also visit your home or workplace, too. The process is fairly quick, inexpensive and is certainly a lot cheaper than repairing and painting the panels!

RUST

Minor rust can be treated with one of many available treatment kits, and should be tackled immediately, as it will only get worse, though major rust and anything other than small dents will require body repair and paintwork.

A-D: the various stages of removing a minor dent in a car's bodywork. Some specialists will come to your home to carry out this work.

Your car's interior will contain various materials, and each will need cleaning in a different way and with different products. Before you start, though, clear the car of all rubbish.

There are numerous car cleaning products available on the market.

To vacuum the carpets, you can either use a 12v cleaner, which plugs into the cigarette lighter in the car, or your household vacuum, which will be more powerful. Treat any stains on the carpets with a proprietary cleaner, possibly using a stiff brush.

With the interior and carpets clean, and possibly shampooed if you have access to a wet or dry vacuum cleaner, you can tackle the seats and any upholstered door panels. Fold any seats that do so and remove any debris from inside the folds before

tackling the seats with the vacuum cleaner. Whether cloth or leather, there are numerous cleaning products available from accessory shops. If you have a wet or dry vacuum it may be worthwhile tackling cloth seats with it, especially if they are grimy, though you will need to leave the car with all the doors open for a few hours for them to dry. Stains on cloth seats should be treated with an automotive fabric cleaner.

Leather seats tend to wear better than cloth, and are unlikely to stain

In some cases, stains on cloth upholstery can just be cleaned with an automotive wipe.

through most spillages. However, dirt can build up in folds in the leather and the grain. Leather cleaners will remove dirt and restore the finish.

Both cloth and leather upholstery can become damaged through neglect or simply wear and tear. Tears in cloth, velour or even headliners can be repaired in situ by a number of companies such as Car Care Systems (www.carcaresystems.com), as can cigarette burns. Cracked dashboards or holes caused by old mobile phone brackets can also be repaired.

There are a number of products available to repair torn leather too, and even some which can fill and bridge gaps. Repairs can often be made to small tears and worn stitching using Superglue. If you have a small tear in leather upholstery,

More stubborn stains are dealt with by spraying and a good rub!

check under the seats to see if there is a small section of excess leather that you can cut off and feed into the tear. Use Superglue to hold it in place. If you are careful, such a repair should last years. Using leather from the car means you get a perfect colour match. Superglue is also ideal for repairing split and torn rubber, such as the weather seals around the doors, but not for repairing cloth or velour.

If part of your car's interior is badly damaged, locate an automotive upholsterer who is able to source matching material, or even a household one perhaps, who may be able to repair any damage.

Plastic door and trim panels should be cleaned either with soap and water or a dedicated cleaner, as not all cleaners are suitable for use on plastic and some could cause damage.

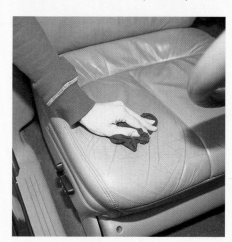

Leather seats will most often just need a wipe with a leather cleaner.

CLEANING THE ENGINE

Although your car will not perform any better with a clean engine bay or engine, cleaning it could help extend the car's life and make any jobs you tackle under the bonnet a less dirty proposition.

Dirt and debris trapped in crevices in the bodywork or on the inner wings are great starting points for rust to gain a foothold, while an engine free from oil and grease, makes it easier to spot any fresh leaks or problems.

There are many de-greasers and engine cleaners on the market. These should be applied, left for a time and then rinsed off. Often a couple of applications will be needed, but with a steam cleaner or pressure washer, one session will be enough. Wherever you clean your engine, place an old sheet under the car to catch the grime that is washed off.

After covering the distributor with a plastic bag and securing it tightly to avoid moisture getting in [A], liberally

apply the de-greaser or engine cleaner [B], concentrating on the dirtier areas. Once it has been allowed to work for the specified time, wash it off using a pressure washer [C]. You may have to tackle some of the more stubborn areas with a brush if using a hosepipe. Finally, remove the protection from the distributor and run the engine for five minutes to thoroughly dry all components.

HOW TO BUY CHEAP PARTS FOR OLD CARS

You may be someone who prefers to maintain your car rather than pay a garage. While many parts should always be bought new, many mechanical parts can be sourced second-hand.

Rather than purchase parts from your main dealer, look through the phone book for an independent spare parts specialist. The prices can be very competitive, especially for service parts such as brake shoes and pads, filters and even some body panels, and they should come with the same guarantees.

Some parts are only available from main dealers. However, even these parts can be obtained from alternative, and cheaper, sources. Scrapyards or breakers' yards have long been the mainstay of do-it-yourself mechanics, and continue to be so today, but increasing legislation and the price of land have ensured that the traditional

> **advice**
>
> ♦ Shop around and get the best price on parts you require.
>
> ♦ Play specialists against each other to get the best price.
>
> ♦ Use a local spares shop for service parts.

scrapyard is almost a thing of the past. The days of wandering around a yard and removing certain car parts have almost disappeared for ever, to the relief of some and the dismay of others!

Although only the larger of such businesses survive, the internet is now a great way of sourcing second-hand parts. Type 'used car parts' into a search engine and websites of the many parts specialists will be at your disposal. These are not individual scrapyards or breakers, but organisations with many breakers on their books, which can search out what you are looking for from their nationwide network. The sites contain forms which you complete, detailing

AUTO ADVICE

Never skimp on safety, even if you do like to save money. You are worth more than a part that was 'really cheap'.

the parts you require. You will then either receive e-mails or phone calls from breakers nationwide who have the part you need. The great thing about this method is that the suppliers can then be played off against each other, until you get the part you want at the price you want to pay! This is a great way to buy second-hand parts – from a distributor to a complete engine – and often you will find the parts have been refurbished or rebuilt before being offered for sale.

You may be able to source whatever parts you want through the weekly classified advertisements in local papers, national publications such as *Exchange and Mart* or other trade parts source magazines.

Sourcing cheap parts for old cars, as well as not-so-old cars is not as hard as you think. For example, a reconditioned distributor for a three-year-old car was sourced via the internet at less than a third of the main dealer price (it was also delivered in two days, whereas the main dealer had to order it specially). A warning, though: safety should not be compromised. Brake parts should always be bought new, as should tyres – even though some tyre fitters may offer part-worn tyres or 'runners'.

Few people now bother scrambling around car breakers' yards in search of spare parts.

SUMMARY

- **Recognising key components**
  Know where to add oil and water
  Know where to check oil levels
  Know where the fuse box is
  Know how to inflate tyres

- **Engine oil**
  Check the oil level regularly
  Change the oil and filter regularly
  Use a funnel when adding oil to
  avoid spillage
  Never overfill the engine oil

- **Coolant**
  Always allow an engine to cool
  before removing the radiator cap
  Never add cold water to an
  overheated engine
  Never remove the cap when hot

- **Power steering**
  Check the fluid level regularly
  Check the drive belt tension
  regularly

- **Brake and clutch fluid**
  Fluid level only drops if there is
  a leak
  Brake fluid is poisonous and
  corrosive to paint
  Do not mix synthetic brake fluid
  with mineral based fluid

- **Manual and automatic gearboxes**
  Manual gearbox oil is not the
  same as engine oil
  Use the correct auto transmission
  fluid for your car

- **Windscreen washers**
  Use screenwash instead of water:
  it will not freeze
  Adjust/clean washer jets with a pin

- **Battery**
  Top up with distilled water
  Do not spill – batteries contain acid
  When replacing the battery,
  remove negative lead first
  Replace the positive lead first
  Remember: re-fit the battery clamp
  Do not leave a battery charger on
  'boost' setting for long

- **Tyres**
  Check the condition and pressure
  of your tyres regularly
  Badly worn tyres are dangerous
  and illegal
  Ensure new tyres have the correct
  identification marks for your vehicle
  Never mix radial and crossply
  tyres
  Never over-inflate tyres

- **Windscreen wipers**
  Check the condition of wiper
  blades regularly
  Replace annually as a matter of
  course
  Never use wipers on a dry screen
  Release frozen wipers before
  switching on

- **Lighting system**
  Check operation and condition of
  all lights periodically
  Check headlight alignment
  Replace blown bulbs immediately
  with an identical type
  Never handle the glass on new
  halogen headlamp bulbs
  Always use the correct bulb for the
  application

- **Mirrors**
  Take care when removing old glass
  from casing
  Correctly align new glass in casing

- **Petrol cap**
  Temporary caps should be
  replaced as soon as possible

- **Frozen or seized door locks**
  Spray penetrating oil into seized
  lock barrels
  Use heat to thaw frozen locks
  Use hot water as a last resort

- **Windscreen damage**
  Windscreen condition is an MOT
  requirement
  Small chips and scratches can be
  repaired

- **Bodywork damage**
  Small scratches and paint scuffs
  can be polished away
  Deeper scratches can be touched
  in with a touch-up stick
  Specialists can remove dents
  without painting

- **Upholstery**
  Ensure you use the correct cleaner
  for each material
  Use Superglue to repair leather
  and plastic

- **Engine bay cleaning**
  Cover the distributor
  Follow instructions on de-greaser
  Use pressure washer or hosepipe

- **Buying cheap parts**
  Shop around and get the best
  price on parts you require
  Play specialists off against each
  other to get the best price
  Use local motor spares shop for
  service parts
  Use the internet to look for
  second-hand parts

5

It is a sad fact of motoring life that no car is 100%
reliable and breakdowns can and do occur. Similarly,
accidents will happen, and driving can be extremely
dangerous if safety is ignored. Consequently, knowing
what to do in the case of a breakdown or accident
will always be an advantage to any motorist.

WHAT TO DO IN THE EVENT OF A BREAKDOWN

So your car has broken down. What do you do? Who should you call? Around 40% of breakdowns happen at home, in which case the urgency is not quite the same as at the roadside.

Firstly, you should get the car out of the path of traffic. If you break down on a motorway, get onto the hard shoulder. Do not stop in a traffic lane, but move to the left before the car stops moving, using the hard shoulder to slow down.

Alert motorists of your plight by placing a warning triangle some way behind your car.

Only 7% of breakdowns occur on a motorway, but if it does happen, get all passengers out of the car and behind a barrier for safety. Stationary cars on the hard shoulder have been known to be hit by passing traffic.

All motorists are advised to stay outside a broken-down vehicle on motorways, but on other roads a lone female driver may feel safer inside the car with the doors locked. Breakdown services usually give priority to women by themselves. If another driver stops to offer help, then use your judgement as to whether you accept or even leave your vehicle.

Alert other motorists to the fact that your car has broken down by using your hazard warning lights or erecting a warning triangle some distance behind your car. It is not obligatory to carry one of these in the UK, but they are required abroad and are a wise investment. They should not be used on a motorway, however; in this instance, use your hazard warning lights.

Now ask yourself if you have any ideas why the car has broken down and if you are able to fix it. For example, has it simply run out of petrol, has it overheated or is it something more serious? If you cannot repair the car, and you are one of the

25 million British motorists who have breakdown cover, you should call your breakdown service provider. On motorways, though, there are emergency phones every mile, with markers and posts to direct you to the nearest one. These markers have a location code, which equate to a certain point on the motorway network, so the breakdown service will be able to locate your vehicle. Even if you do not have breakdown cover, use the emergency phones. You will have to pay, but a recovery vehicle will be called to

Once your breakdown service has been called, a mechanic will be sent out to repair the vehicle. Depending on the type of cover you have, if it cannot be fixed, a recovery vehicle will usually be sent to transport the car to your destination or a garage. An estimated one third of broken down cars require towing to a garage.

If you are not on a motorway, and you are not a member of any breakdown service, you will either have to locate a local garage or telephone a mechanic for assistance.

Emergency breakdown assistance is great for peace of mind, especially on long journeys.

remove your car from the motorway. Once off the motorway, you will have to arrange repair or recovery yourself. If you frequently drive long distances, then it is definitely worthwhile taking out breakdown cover.

Breaking down almost always happens at the most inopportune moment and is a stressful and inconvenient occurrence. Anything that can be done to make it more bearable can only help matters.

There are certain items you should always carry in your vehicle, and others that you should take on longer journeys, in case of breakdowns.

Essential items should include a basic tool kit, torch and petrol can. Even if your mechanical knowledge is limited,

A warning triangle, a first aid kit and a set of spare bulbs are mandatory when travelling abroad.

AUTO ADVICE
If you are a paid-up member of a motoring organisation, always carry their phone number in your car!

being stranded when something as simple as a screwdriver or correct size spanner could get you out of trouble is no fun. Likewise, breaking down at night and knowing you could fix the problem if only you had a torch in the car is equally as frustrating. As for running out of petrol and having to buy a can once you finally reach a petrol station,

or worse still the garage not having any cans in stock, wouldn't it be easier if you kept one in the boot?

On longer journeys and especially during the winter, a blanket, drinking water, a map and a flask containing a hot drink are good items to pack, as is making sure that your mobile phone is fully charged up. You will be thankful for all of these extra items if you became stranded or even while waiting for the breakdown organisation to arrive. In fact, it is a good idea to carry a mobile phone and drinking water with you even on short journeys.

If you are mechanically inclined, you may want to carry a few spares, or at least items that could facilitate repairs, such as insulating tape,

stationary and have broken down; a complete bulb set: this means you can change any blown bulbs immediately; and finally, a basic first aid kit: this may come in useful, even if it is just a plaster for a small cut.

Check your car has a jack, a jack handle and wheelbrace, as well as a good, inflated spare tyre, too. There is nothing worse than getting a puncture, only to find you cannot change the

wheel or that the spare is also flat! A good set of jump leads for use if the car has a flat battery is a worthwhile purchase, although checking your battery is in top condition (see page 64), especially before winter, is an advisable precaution.

hose clips, cable ties, fuses, an alternator belt and bungees. Keeping a fire extinguisher in the car is also a sound idea.

If you travel abroad, even in Europe, you are obliged by law to carry the following items in your vehicle – although it is advisable to carry them at all times anyway: an emergency warning triangle – this warns motorists who are driving towards your car that you are

emergency kit checklist

- Jack and wheelbrace
- Basic tool kit
- Torch
- Petrol can
- Blanket
- Drinks
- Map
- Warning triangle
- Spare bulbs
- First aid kit
- Spares
- Cable ties, tape and bungees
- Jump leads

DEALING WITH A FLAT BATTERY

Flat batteries mainly occur at the car owner's home or place of work, where the vehicle has been parked for a period of time, and usually an electrical device has been left switched on.

Flat batteries are the number one cause of call-outs, according to motoring organisations. A major cause is the headlights being switched on in the dark or murky conditions in the morning, then forgotten about as the light improves. Leaving the lights on for a couple of hours will drain the battery

Position a second car close to the one with the flat battery, and use jump leads to restart.

sufficiently for it not to be able to start the car.

Until recently, the easiest way to start a car with a flat battery was to 'jump start' it using jump leads and another car, but with the availability of 'power packs', it is now even easier – provided you have a fully charged power pack to hand, that is! If you call one of the motoring organisations, they will most likely use a power pack to start your car (see page 67), as using jump leads requires manoeuvring a second car close to yours, something that may not be possible at the side of a road, for instance.

If you have to jump start a vehicle with a flat battery, and do not own a power pack, position a second vehicle so that the batteries are as close together as possible. Switch off the ignition on both cars and apply the handbrake. Ensuring that the ends of the jump leads do not come into contact with any part of either vehicle's bodywork, connect one end of the red lead to the positive

Breakdown organisations commonly use a power pack to restart a flat battery.

of the second vehicle and maintain a fast idle speed. The vehicle with the flat battery can now also be started.

Finally, turn off the second vehicle's ignition and disconnect the jump leads in the reverse order of connection. If the engine of the vehicle with the flat battery dies when the leads are disconnected, the alternator is not charging the battery, and the fitting of a replacement battery will only last until that too drains. Unfortunately, this means that a new alternator is needed. Once the engine of the vehicle with the flat battery has started, the car should be driven for a distance of around 20 miles to fully charge the battery, using the minimum of electrical equipment – so turn off any lights, stereo or heating.

terminal of the flat battery, and the other end to the positive terminal of the second vehicle. Connect the black lead to the negative terminal of the battery on the second vehicle, and the other end of this lead, if possible, to a metal bracket or the earthing strap of the engine on the vehicle with the flat battery. If not possible or you are unsure, connect the black lead to the negative terminal of the flat battery.

Making sure both leads are well away from any moving parts, such as fans or drivebelts, start the engine

advice

- Owning a charged power pack means you do not have to rely on another vehicle to jump start your car.

- Ensure you connect any jump leads the correct way round.

- Never let jump leads touch any bodywork or other metal parts.

- Keep jump leads away from fans and drivebelts.

- Once started, drive for some distance to fully charge the battery.

CHANGING A WHEEL

Closely following flat batteries as a cause of breakdowns, motoring organisations list punctures and changing wheels as their second largest reason for callouts.

If you have to change a wheel, remove the spare wheel from the car before you start. There are two reasons for this: firstly, it may also be flat and secondly, you should avoid disturbing the vehicle once it is raised (jacked up). Before you begin to jack up the car, use the wheel brace to loosen the wheel nuts on the wheel to be changed. Loosen each one only half a turn anti-clockwise [A]; if you do not do this now, it will be near impossible once the wheel is raised off the ground. With the ignition off, the handbrake on and the car on

USING A JACK

Only ever jack up a car on a firm, level surface, as far away from the edge of the road as possible.
1 Remove the jack from the boot of the car and push it into position. **2** Secure the mounting point of the jack into the jacking point on the car's chassis. **3** Wind, or pump up the jack, according to its type.

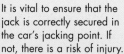

It is vital to ensure that the jack is correctly secured in the car's jacking point. If not, there is a risk of injury.

as level ground as you can find – bearing in mind you may be changing the wheel at the side of the road – place the jack under a recommended jacking point (consult your handbook). This will most likely be underneath the vehicle just behind

a front wheel [B] and in front of a rear wheel.

Now you can take off the wheel nuts and then remove the wheel, taking care not to place any part of your body underneath the vehicle. Once the wheel with the flat tyre is off, you may wish to slide it halfway under the car as a precautionary measure [C], though not so you cannot fit the spare wheel. In the unlikely event that the jack should give way, the car will come to rest on top of the wheel without damaging any mechanical parts or more importantly, any part of you.

Fit the spare wheel in the reverse order of removal [D] and tighten the nuts clockwise as much as possible before removing the old wheel from

under the car and releasing the jack. Then tighten the wheel nuts again once the wheel is on the ground. Sometimes wheel nuts can be very hard to undo, as they may have previously been put on at a garage using a pneumatic air wrench, or they

may simply be rusted on. If possible, you should smear a little anti-seize compound or grease onto the studs before replacing the nuts. If you are not confident you have tightened the nuts sufficiently using the wheel brace, have them checked at a garage at the earliest opportunity.

advice

- Check you have a jack, handle, wheel brace and spare wheel in your vehicle.

- Locking wheel nuts require an adaptor. Ensure you have one.

- Wheel nuts should be tightened to the settings specified in your car's handbook. If they are any tighter, you may not be able to undo them with a wheel brace and will need to have them removed at a garage with specialist equipment.

DEALING WITH A FLOODED ENGINE/ RUNNING OUT OF PETROL

A 'flooded engine' is what happens when the engine receives too much neat petrol, instead of the perfectly mixed vapour needed for combustion.

The presence of liquid petrol in the cylinder makes the spark plug wet, which cannot then produce a spark to ignite the fuel.

A flooded engine is often caused by the driver 'pumping' the accelerator pedal while turning the ignition key. With carburettor-equipped vehicles, this will cause neat petrol to enter the combustion chambers; on a fuel-injected engine, this confuses the computer and is likely to lead to excess fuel entering the engine cylinders.

If the engine does not start after several tries, press the accelerator pedal to the floor, keep it there, then turn the key again. If this fails to work after a few attempts, leave it for 15 minutes then try again. If this still does not work, you may have to remove the spark plugs and dry them, or call a mechanic or breakdown service.

Another fuel problem is running out of the stuff! Check your fuel gauge on the dashboard with the ignition lights on but before you start the engine; if the gauge reads empty, you need to

If you know you have run out of fuel, then your motoring organisation can bring some to you.

add petrol before starting the engine. You may have to turn the engine over several times to draw fuel through the system. Try to avoid running out of fuel; it causes dirt and debris at the bottom of the fuel tank to be drawn through the system, causing further problems. Always carry a petrol can in the boot.

DEALING WITH OVERHEATING

Most of us have witnessed overheating cars on the side of the road, with their bonnets up and steam gushing forth from the engine bay, usually in the summer months in traffic jams.

There are several possible causes for overheating; a lack of coolant is one. If the level has suddenly dropped, is there a leak? If the engine head gasket has failed, there will be mayonnaise-type deposits in the coolant and the car will lack power. Drive the car no further; call a mechanic.

Perhaps the fan is faulty. Most cars have electrically operated fans, activated by a heat sensitive switch when the coolant temperature rises. If they fail to turn on, the car overheats.

The thermostat may be seized. This controls the coolant flow, reducing flow in a cold engine to enable it to warm up more rapidly, then opening as the temperature rises. If it sticks in its closed position, the car will overheat. Very carefully touch the rubber hose that exits from the top of the radiator. If cold, the thermostat is likely to be stuck. But this could also indicate a failed coolant pump. Usually a failed pump will result in a serious leak. If the pump is driven by a belt, which has broken, the pump will simply not turn, though no leak will be evident.

The most common cause is a combination of coolant level that has been allowed to drop, sitting stationary in traffic with no airflow through the radiator, usually in hot weather, and a faulty fan. If your temperature gauge is creeping up towards the red zone, and showing no signs of going back down, turn the heater on to maximum, which should help dissipate some heat. Once the engine becomes too hot, pull over. Let it cool to the touch, and if you have any water, refill the coolant system.

AUTO ADVICE

Let your car's temperature drop before adding coolant, as adding cold water to a hot system could result in damage.

If the temperature gauge rises suddenly, turn the heater on to maximum to release some heat.

WHAT TO DO IN THE EVENT OF AN ACCIDENT

Accidents involving motor vehicles, however minor, are always unpleasant, but the main thing to remember in any accident situation is not to panic.

No matter how precious they are to their owners, cars are only metal objects, and the safety of human life should always take top priority after an accident.

If you are involved in an accident that causes damage or injury to people, domesticated animals (or deer, as they are owned by the Crown), another vehicle or roadside fixtures, you are duty bound by law to stop at the scene and report the incident to the police as soon as possible. Definitely do this within 24 hours, as failure to report an accident is a serious offence.

Following an accident, switch the ignition off in all vehicles involved, and use any means necessary to warn oncoming traffic of the danger, such as placing warning triangles in the road or sending someone to signal traffic

Once details have been exchanged, your car may need help to get it on its way.

to slow down. As there is a risk of petrol leakages, keep smokers away from any wreckage. At the scene, call for an ambulance if anyone involved requires urgent medical attention, or call the police if the road is blocked or someone involved leaves the scene without giving their details. You should call the fire brigade if there is a risk of fire or serious fuel spillage occurs.

If the vehicles involved can be moved to the side of the road, and in most accidents they can be, do so, as it will enable passing traffic to flow freely. Never stop in the outside lane

AUTO ADVICE

Note whether any drivers were talking on mobile phones or if they were not wearing seatbelts.

of a motorway after an accident, but try and manoeuvre to the hard shoulder, reducing the risk of further collisions and damage to you, your vehicle or someone else.

Record the name, address and vehicle registration of any witnesses, as this could be important later during insurance claims. Exchange details with any other drivers involved (see page 106 for further details). Once these essential details have been noted, it is wise to record as many other details as you can, as soon as possible. Describe any injuries that were caused, not just to you, and

advice

- Stop after an accident.

- Exchange details with other drivers or anyone having reasonable grounds for asking, such as owners of parked cars or property damaged in the accident.

- Acquire witnesses' details.

- Make a sketch or take photographs.

record details of any damage to vehicles. Note the location, date and time of the accident, the type of road, direction of travel, collision points, vehicle positions, the weather and road conditions, as well as whether it occurred in daylight or not. By the time the details of some winter accidents are processed by insurance companies, they may not consider that

Breakdown organisations will come and tow your vehicle to a garage for repairs.

an accident at 4pm, for instance, would have happened after dark.

Any skid marks on the road should be noted, as well as the speed of all vehicles involved. If you keep a camera in your car, take pictures at the scene. Whether you have taken photographs or not, draw a sketch of the accident, including as many details as possible. See the following page for more details on this.

If the other driver is threatening, call the police to the scene and allow them to deal with the situation.

EXCHANGING DETAILS/ DRAWING A SKETCH

Unless you are very fortunate, most accidents will involve some damage to your vehicle and at least one other. There is also a risk of damaging property belonging to a third party.

Whether the insurance company of the person at fault for the accident is to pay, or whether it will be dealt with privately, it is still a legal requirement for everyone involved in the accident to exchange details. Obviously, this should be done after the safety of everyone involved has been secured, and the vehicles are moved to prevent causing any obstruction. If there were no other moving vehicles involved, but you hit a building, road sign or parked car, you should give your particulars to anyone having 'reasonable grounds to ask', for example, the owner of the property you have damaged. In the case of a road sign, the police should be called.

You should exchange names and addresses, telephone numbers and vehicle registrations, including the names and addresses of any witnesses. If you have the details with you, you may also wish to exchange insurance company details and your policy numbers, although you are

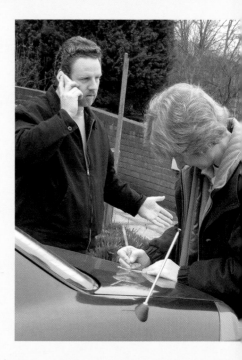

You are legally required to exchange details at the scene of any accident.

only obliged to do so if anyone has been hurt in the accident. Another driver cannot demand to see your insurance details or driving licence, but a police officer can.

If another driver refuses to tell you their name or address, or you feel they may have committed a crime, such as driving while under the influence of drink or driving a stolen car, you should call the police immediately.

DRAWING A ROUGH SKETCH

As soon as possible after the accident you should sketch as many details as you can remember. Any insurance form you complete will ask for a plan of the accident, and you will recall more details if you do this immediately. Draw a plan of the road layout where the accident occurred, as if viewed from above, including details such as the position of all vehicles on the road, the width of the road and any road signs.

AUTO ADVICE

If you keep a camera with you, photographs of the scene will enhance any sketch.

The direction that the cars involved were travelling in, as well as skid marks and collision points, should be included, and street names will also be helpful. You do not need to make the drawing detailed – simple rectangles will suffice to depict the cars, as shown in the sketch below – just as long as the drawing gives a clear representation of the road layout and how the accident happened.

Do not worry about your artistic ability, just as long as the drawing is clear and unambiguous.

ACCIDENT EMERGENCY FIRST AID

Following an accident, you should only administer first aid if you have been properly trained to do so, but there are a number of things you can do to help.

Ensure the engines of all cars involved are switched off and inform any emergency services required. You can do this yourself or ask any witnesses or bystanders instead. Then you can try to help any people involved in the accident.

Do not move any casualties who are still in their vehicles unless there is a serious risk to their safety, such as fire. Never remove a motorcyclist's helmet unless absolutely essential, as you could seriously aggravate their injuries. Do not let any casualties eat

AUTO ADVICE Basic first aid could help you save someone's life, so think about going along to a local training course.

or drink until they have been examined by qualified medical staff.

You can prevent any casualties from getting cold, and make them as comfortable as possible until help arrives, but avoid any unnecessary movement, as they may have injuries that neither they nor you are aware of. Offer reassurance and stay with them until professional help arrives at the scene.

While this is in no way meant as a first aid guide, the following 'ABC of first aid' may help in serious situations.

A – Airway Check for and remove any obstructions to improve breathing. The casualty may simply be choking on their own tongue or may have been eating at the time of the accident.

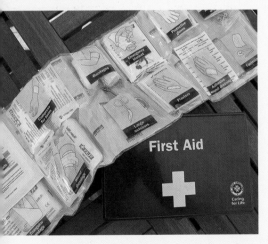

Although it is not yet obligatory to keep one in a car in the UK, a first aid kit is always a good idea.

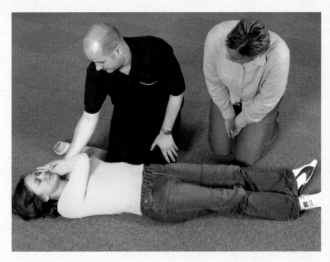

Organisations such as St John Ambulance offer training courses in first aid.

B – Breathing If the casualty is still not breathing once you have cleared their airway, tilt their heads backwards gently, pinch their nostrils to prevent air escaping and blow into their mouth until their chest rises. Repeat this procedure – sometimes referred to as the 'kiss of life' – every four seconds until they can breathe unaided.

C – Circulation Maintain circulation by preventing blood loss. If the casualty is injured and bleeding, apply firm pressure on the wound using the cleanest material available, without disturbing any object that has entered the wound. Use hand pressure to stem any bleeding, then secure whatever material you have used with a bandage or similar. Raise the injured part of the body to reduce the bleeding, though if it is a limb, ensure it is not broken first.

All the above would obviously be made simpler with a first aid kit. Although it is a requirement for motorists in continental Europe, you are not legally obliged to carry a first aid kit in your car in the UK at the present time, but it is advisable. You may have been trained in basic first aid through your job, but further training is available from organisations such as the British Red Cross, St John Ambulance Association or even your local ambulance service.

first aid dos and don'ts

- **DO** call emergency services immediately.
- **DON'T** move casualties unless imperative.
- **DO** keep casualties warm and reassured.
- **DON'T** remove motorcyclists' helmets.
- **DO** ensure casualties can breathe.
- **DO** try to stem any bleeding.

SUMMARY

- **Breakdown**
  Remove your vehicle from the
  traffic flow
  Activate hazard warning lights
  Can you repair the vehicle?
  Call motoring organisation

- **Emergency kit**
  Ensure you are fully prepared in
  case of breakdowns, especially if
  travelling long distances

- **Flat battery**
  Connect jump leads the correct
  way round
  Once started, drive for some
  distance to fully charge the battery
  Consider buying a power pack

- **Changing a wheel**
  Does your car have a jack, handle,
  wheel brace and spare wheel?
  Do wheel nuts require an adaptor?
  Loosen the wheel nuts before
  jacking the vehicle
  Ensure the vehicle cannot fall on
  you at any time

- **Flooded engine**
  Press accelerator to floor and
  turn key

  Leave for 15 minutes and try again
  Remove and clean spark plugs

- **Running out of petrol**
  Carry petrol can in boot of car
  Turn engine in ten second bursts to
  draw new fuel through system

- **Overheating**
  Never remove the coolant cap until
  the temperature drops
  Never fill a hot coolant system with
  cold water

- **Accident**
  Stop after an accident
  Exchange details with other drivers
  Acquire witnesses details
  Make a sketch or take photographs

- **Exchanging details**
  Exchange names, addresses,
  telephone numbers and vehicle
  registrations

- **Emergency first aid**
  Call emergency services
  immediately
  Do not move casualties unless
  absolutely essential
  Keep casualties warm, and reassured

6

safety & security

Car safety and security are of paramount importance
to all automotive manufacturers and should be to the
motorist, as well. Car crime has reached record levels in
recent years and with the roads ever more crowded with
vehicles, driving has never been more hazardous.

CAR SAFETY AND SECURITY

Car security is an increasingly serious issue. In this chapter, we take a look at alarms and security devices, and how you can try to stop your car becoming an attractive target for thieves.

Over 25% of all crimes are car-related crimes, whether they are car thefts or items stolen from cars. Car safety is also important, with two very different aspects of safety to consider. Firstly, how safe is your car, and secondly do you do everything you can to ensure your personal safety while driving?

All new vehicles are subject to safety checks and strict regulations. Independent tests are also carried out to see how well different models fare in crash tests. When considering a new car, compare test results. Crumple zones are built in to car structures at the design stage. This means that although the vehicle may be damaged beyond economical repair after a crash, the occupants may well survive unscathed. Check to see whether the vehicle has driver and passenger airbags, side airbags, side impact protection, seat belt tensioners and adjustable headrests.

Does the car have traction control (a device which prevents driven wheels from spinning in wet or slippery conditions), anti-lock brakes (ABS) and is the stability known to be good? The safety features built in to a car can contribute to it not being involved in an accident in the first place. ABS will ensure you retain the ability to steer, even on loose or slippery surfaces, where non-ABS equipped vehicles would skid or slide. Tall cars, such as four wheel drive vehicles, have a higher centre of gravity and are more

Cars are tested for performance during crash scenarios. Comparing results will help you make a choice on safety issues.

unstable than a normal car that is much lower to the ground.

When it comes to personal safety there are numerous issues, from driving while tired to threats of physical violence from other drivers. If you feel tired it is best not to set out, particularly on a motorway journey, where you will not be changing gear, braking or much else except for steering. If you do decide to make the journey, do not set cruise control if you have it, but do open a window and turn the heater down or off.

Locking all the doors while driving is a wise precaution that few people bother with, yet the number of incidents involving car-jacking is on the increase. Leaving valuables on show is an invitation to thieves.

If you become involved in a road rage incident, stay calm and do not be drawn into a confrontation. Women, especially, are likely to feel intimidated by such an experience, but staying calm, not smiling and remaining

Do not leave any valuables on show, especially when you are not in the car.

confident can help diffuse the situation. Even if the row was not your fault, simply backing down can often resolve the dispute. If in doubt, do not get out of the car, keep the doors locked, and do not open the window. Keep your mobile phone to hand and make it clear to any aggressor that you will call for help if the situation escalates.

There are now courses designed specifically for women and the danger they may face on the roads. From basic jobs such as changing a wheel, through techniques for avoiding confrontations to self defence, the courses are intended to reduce the number of women who feel vulnerable in a car, and make them less likely to be stranded alone with a minor problem such as a flat tyre.

AUTO ADVICE

Buy a car that has a good safety record and do not leave any valuables on show.

As well as protecting your pride and joy, and offering peace of mind, fitting an alarm to your car is one of the few things you can do to actually lower your insurance premium.

Fitting an alarm yourself is possible but you will most likely have to have it professionally installed – and Thatcham approved – to make any difference to your insurance company. Thatcham is the Motor Industry Repair Research Centre at Thatcham in Berkshire that issues rating categories for security devices. A Thatcham-approved category means the device has passed strict tests and is fully approved.

There are cheap alarms and expensive alarms: you basically get what you pay for. Some offer better protection than others, so it really

AUTO ADVICE

If you cannot afford an alarm, a flashing LED on your dashboard is a useful alternative for deterring would-be thieves.

depends on how secure you want your car to be and what you are trying to protect. A good quality basic alarm that perhaps has a two stage shock feature, where it will not go off if the car is accidentally knocked, but will activate after a major shock or repeated shocks, is probably all that most people will require.

Watch out if your alarm suddenly starts repeatedly activating when it has not done so before. Some thieves deliberately set the alarm off repeatedly, so that you end up not re-setting it. Bearing in mind the speed with which thieves can get into and drive away most models, fitting an alarm makes sense.

If you decide to fit a DIY alarm yourself, make sure it is Thatcham approved.

SECURITY DEVICES

You can go a long way towards preventing yourself from becoming a victim of car crime by fitting some form of mechanical immobiliser, which will be a forceful deterrent to a would-be thief.

Most thieves will not worry about how they enter your car, and can smash a window and gain entry in a matter of seconds. Consequently, any immobiliser you fit should act as both a physical obstacle and a visual deterrent. Cheaper immobilisers are available, but a mid-range model, especially if it is obvious from outside the car, will cause a thief to think twice. A bright yellow rod through your steering wheel will certainly put off any casual thief.

One of the main problems with mechanical immobilisers is that they are not used as frequently as they should be. No matter how good the product is, it is useless if it remains in the boot or on the back seat.

Look for something that is highly visible, easy to use and theft resistant. This limits the search to something that fits on the steering wheel or possibly joins the handbrake to the gear lever. While wheel clamps are good protection for caravans or cars that are not in daily use, they are almost universally awkward to fit and bulky to carry around.

Wheel clamps are great for cars or caravans that are rarely used, but can be tricky to fit.

This steering wheel immobiliser, obvious from outside the car, is a sight to deter most thieves.

AIRBAGS AND PASSENGER PROTECTION SYSTEMS

Virtually all modern cars come with a driver airbag as standard equipment, with many also offering an airbag for the front seat passenger.

An airbag is triggered when an electronic sensor decides that deceleration has been caused by an impact. The airbag is released and rapidly fills with a gas, then begins to deflate immediately. This is so it can absorb much of the impact and add to the protection offered by seat belts. The car occupants can then escape quickly.

An airbag only works once, and if you have had one activated it will need replacing, which is definitely not a DIY job. They also only last safely for around ten years, and again will need replacing by an authorised fitter. If the airbag warning light illuminates on your dashboard, the system should be checked immediately.

Some cars also have side impact airbags in the door pillars or seats, while many more have side impact protection bars inside the doors, which reduce the amount the door will intrude into the passenger cabin in the event of a side impact.

Modern cars are designed to collapse around the passenger compartment, which extensively damages the structure of the car, but saves the lives of the occupants in many cases.

AUTO ADVICE

Small children or elderly people should not sit in the front passenger seat of a car with a passenger airbag.

Airbags are not filled with air, but gas, which is triggered on impact to inflate the bags.

SEAT BELTS

It is over 20 years since the wearing of seat belts first became compulsory in the UK, and we often take them for granted. Probably the only time they get checked is at the annual MOT test.

Spend a couple of minutes checking that the webbing of the belts is not frayed or twisted, and that they retract properly. All modern cars are equipped with inertia reel seat belts. These normally allow the belt to be pulled from the reel, while 'locking up' in the event of a crash, owing to the inertia. If you pull suddenly on the shoulder belt, it should lock. If not, the belt is faulty and will need replacing.

Inertia reel seat belts should be replaced after any accident, especially if your car is fitted with seat belt tensioners on the front seat

Manufacturers undertake extensive tests with dummies before letting humans use their belts.

belts. These are designed to pull the belt tight around the passenger in the event of impact, but if the tensioner mechanism is activated, it should be replaced.

For all passengers in seats without airbags, the seat belts are the only form of protection in an accident, so they should be checked and worn at all times. Young children should sit on booster seats if required and child seats should be mounted properly. Children should never be allowed to sit on a passenger's lap or travel without suitable belt restraints.

Seat belts can save lives, so check that they retract properly and are not frayed or worn.

CHILD SEATS

Small children should always be seated in dedicated child seats and not on an adult's lap or restrained by an adult seat belt alone. It is just not possible to hold onto a child in an accident.

Child seats must always be fitted properly; if the seat can move around, then the child is just strapped into something that is going to move around the cabin in an accident.

Child seats are secured using the adult seat belt, and it may take a few tries to fit it properly. There should be no excessive movement in any direction; if you are at all unhappy with the way a child seat fits into your car, try a different design of seat with differently placed mountings.

In the case of seats for smaller children, the adult belt holds the seat in place, with a harness in the seat to restrain the child. With booster seats and cushions, the adult belt also

Infant seats are secured by the adult belt, but also have a harness to restrain the child.

A baby seat is secured with the seat belt and the baby faces towards the rear of the car.

child seats

- When choosing a child seat, select one that is suitable for the child's weight and size as well as their age. Baby seats, child seats, booster seats and booster cushions should all carry an 'E' mark or British Standard 'Kite' mark to show they meet the required standards.

- Do not be tempted to buy a second-hand child seat, as its history will be unknown and it may be damaged or have parts missing of which you will not be aware. If it comes without any instructions, you will not know how to correctly fit it to your car or, more importantly, it may not meet the latest safety standards.

AUTO ADVICE

Always carry children in a car seat and ensure you have the correct seat for your child's size and weight.

restrains the child. You should not be able to slide more than a couple of fingers under the harness with the child strapped in.

The first child seat you are likely to buy will be a baby seat. These are held in place by the adult seat belt, so that the baby faces towards the rear of the car. In the event of an accident, this means that the baby is supported by its whole back and not just the seat's harness. It is also safer for a baby's weak neck. Child seats, and especially rear facing ones, should not be fitted in the front seat of any vehicle with a front passenger airbag, as serious injuries may result in the event of the airbag being activated.

The next type of seat will be for an infant, which will last to the age of around four, depending on the weight of the child. Only use this type of seat once your child can sit unaided. These are forward facing seats, again secured by the adult belts, and still with a harness to restrain the child.

Some also have their own mounting straps. The harness in the seat should be of the 'five point' type, with a pair of shoulder straps coming to the centre clasp and then going down to either side of the seat, and a crotch strap to prevent the child from sliding forward.

When your child outgrows a child seat, you will need a booster seat. This has no harness, but uses the adult belt to restrain the child. The seat has guides, on both sides of the base and at shoulder height, through which the seat belt should pass, correctly positioning the child. Booster seats are often available with removable back sections, turning them into booster cushions as the child gets older.

Booster seats do not have a harness but use guides through which to pass the seat belt.

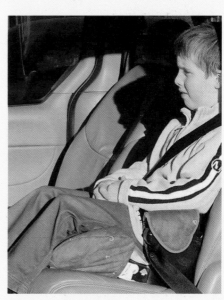

FIRE!

It is worth bearing in mind that if all the safety measures implemented by manufacturers were taken away, a car would be little more than a mobile bomb.

During the late 1970s, many American Ford Pintos exploded when hit by another car from behind, allegedly because their fuel tanks simply could not withstand collisions. It is not too unusual to see old Volkswagen Beetles on fire on the roads, as they are notorious for fuel leaks in the engine bay as they age, which then ignite on the hot motor. Even six year old Chryslers were recalled in 2002 for a fault with a fuel pipe.

Combine petrol, accidents and a simple method of ignition – sparks from colliding metal, hot engines, connecting jump leads or even

Carrying a fire extinguisher in the car is a thoroughly sensible precaution to take.

cigarettes – and it is surprising more accidents do not end in flames. Carrying a fire extinguisher will help if a fire breaks out, and mounting it within easy reach of the driver is a good idea. If it is in the boot, you may not even be able to reach it.

However, not only accidents result in fires. Letting fuel spill onto a hot motor can start a fire, as can smoking near a car while it is undergoing mechanical work. Sparks from a grinder, connecting a battery or even a pilot light in an external appliance could all ignite fumes. Believe it or not, so can mobile phones, when used in garages or on petrol station forecourts. The most common cause of automotive fires, however, is an electrical short circuit or failure.

A fire in a car, caused either by an accident or an electrical fault, can be disastrous.

OTHER SECURITY MEASURES

Since 1998, all new cars have been fitted as standard with electronic immobilisers by manufacturers. But is there anything else that vehicle owners can do or buy to combat car crime?

Anti-theft deadlocks are fitted on many cars, although they are not always used: do *you* lock your car when paying for fuel? If you don't, such 'contributory negligence', as it is termed, means you will not be paid by the insurance company should your car be stolen in such circumstances. Manufacturers have vastly improved door locks on cars over the past few years, making it harder to access the mechanisms via the window rubbers, and most lock knobs are now all but impossible to lift with a coat hanger jammed between the door window

AUTO ADVICE

Garaging a car at night greatly reduces the likelihood of it being stolen – but lock the garage, as well as the car!

frame and the bodywork. However, ultimately, the responsibility for car security lies with the owner.

In addition to alarms and security devices, you can have windows and light lenses etched with your car's registration number, making it harder to change the vehicle's identity or for a thief to sell on the car's lights and glass. Tougher security glass can make it harder to smash windows to gain entry – a popular method for opportunist thieves – and locking wheel nuts will deter alloy wheel thieves. Finally, a tracking device will not stop your car from being stolen, but it will increase the chances of you getting it back again.

Never leave your keys in the ignition – especially when you go to pay for fuel.

SUMMARY

- **Safety and security**
  Buy a car with a good safety record
  Do not drive when tired
  Lock all doors whilst driving
  Do not leave valuables on show
  Avoid road rage incidents

- **Alarms**
  Fitting an alarm could reduce
  insurance premiums
  Make sure an alarm is Thatcham
  approved
  Visit www.vsib.co.uk for a list of
  accredited Thatcham-approved fitters
  Always reset alarms and
  investigate cause of trigger

- **Safety devices**
  Choose a highly visible, easy to
  use immobiliser
  Check consumer reports for the
  best buy
  Ensure a wheel clamp will fit your car

- **Airbags and protection
  systems**
  Never tamper with an unreleased
  airbag
  Avoid using heat or hammering if
  making repairs near steering wheel
  Never have a child seat where a
  front passenger airbag is fitted

- **Seat belts**
  Check seat belts for fraying and
  twists
  Pull on shoulder belts to check
  locking mechanism
  Replace any belts with tensioner
  mechanisms after a collision

- **Child seats**
  Always carry children in a
  dedicated car seat
  Never carry a child on an adult's
  lap, even for short journeys
  Choose a seat with an easily
  adjustable harness
  Ensure you have the correct seat
  for your child's size and weight
  Ensure any child seat is properly fitted

- **Fire**
  Carry a fire extinguisher near the
  driver's seat
  Check for fuel leaks and repair
  immediately
  If you smell petrol, don't smoke
  and switch off your engine

- **Security measures**
  Lock your car at all times
  Use security devices and alarms
  Have your windows etched
  Fit locking wheelnuts to alloy wheels

7

You have had the lessons to enable you to pass the driving test. What more do you need to know? There are many aspects of driving that you will only come across when you experience them for the first time or that need more practice, such as driving in wet or icy conditions.

CORRECT DRIVING POSITION

You may not realise it, but the way your seat and steering column is adjusted, and the position you subsequently adopt in your vehicle, can affect the way you drive. Your driving position can also have an effect on your stress levels in the vehicle.

Your seat should obviously be in the most comfortable position for you, but it also needs to fulfil a few other criteria. It should support your whole back, with particular attention to your lower back. Most modern cars have adjustable lumbar supports, which should be adjusted so you feel slight pressure, rather than a lump. Your arms should be slightly bent to minimise fatigue and tension, so adjust the seat backwards or forwards or recline the backrest to find the optimum position.

The steering wheel should be positioned so that your hands are lower than your shoulders. Most cars have adjustable steering columns for this. You may also be able to slide the steering wheel to and from your body to find the perfect position.

All modern cars have headrests. Adjust them so that they are level with the base of your skull. This is vital should you have an accident.

Finally, check you can reach all the controls as well as the pedals once your seat belt is on.

Adopting the correct driving position will keep you fresh, attentive and comfortable in the car.

You should be able to reach all the controls in your car safely and comfortably.

DRIVING AWARENESS

Driver error is a major cause of accidents. Your level of awareness while driving is extremely important, and while modern cars contain all manner of safety devices, they also have distractions such as music, satellite navigation and a myriad of controls.

Before starting a journey, ensure that you can see properly in all mirrors and through all windows, especially in the winter months, when the glass can become steamed up or iced over. It may sound obvious, but concentrate at all times and anticipate what other road users may be about to do. It is easy for your concentration to lapse, especially on a motorway, and this is the most likely place for drivers to fall asleep behind the wheel.

On a motorway, if you feel tired, pull off at the next junction or service area, not the hard shoulder. A short walk in the fresh air may help, or

Driver fatigue causes numerous traffic accidents, particularly on motorways.

even a short nap can be effective in combating tiredness.

Whatever the type of road, drive at a safe speed to suit the conditions, and slow down in bad weather. Pay particular attention when traffic becomes heavy, and leave plenty of space to brake between your vehicle and that in front.

'Road rage' is on the increase, but if you find yourself becoming annoyed by other drivers, stay calm and drive away as soon as you can (see page 113).

driver awareness dos & don'ts

▶ **DO** plan your trip to include rest breaks and try not to drive for more than two hours at a time without a break.

▶ **DON'T** drive too fast and too close to the car in front, especially on a motorway: this is the cause of most multiple vehicle crashes.

▶ **DON'T** speed up if you are followed, but drive to a police station or busy area. If you have a mobile phone, call for help.

THE ART OF CAR CONTROL

Passing a driving test may prove that you are safe and competent enough to drive a car, but until you experience a skid or collision as a driver, you cannot be fully prepared for what will happen. However, you can prepare to a certain extent.

Most people will have heard how they should 'steer in the direction of the skid' if they start to skid, but what does that actually mean? If the rear end of the vehicle starts to skid towards the right, it means you should steer to the right, keeping the front wheels pointed in the original direction of travel, and at the same time easing off the accelerator and brake. This should correct the skid.

If, under heavy braking, the wheels start to skid in a straight line – in an emergency stop situation, for example – try to come off the brake pedal and quickly re-apply it, but less vigorously.

AUTO ADVICE

Maintain smooth, minimal steering movements and exercise responsibility while driving.

Stopping will take longer than normal, and you may have to apply the brakes a number of times (known as cadence braking), but it will help you regain some control over the steering and stop you skidding into other vehicles or people.

Learning to control a skid or slide takes practice, and while there are purpose-built skidpans around, they are mainly for use by professional drivers. However, you can

The golden rule for controlling a skid is to steer into it, but only practice or an actual experience will show you how.

Learn to control skids and slides at a karting track – and have a fun day out as well!

always bear in mind the safety of other road users.

Car control is not just about knowing what to do when things go wrong, however. Having control of a vehicle is as much about avoiding such situations. Steering movements should be kept to a minimum and be 'fluid' to maintain balance. Corners should be approached without excess speed, then power increased on the exit as the steering is straightened.

Finally, tyres in good condition at the correct pressure, and functioning shock absorbers and suspension, will help any car's handling.

gain valuable experience in the art of car control by practising on private land or more easily, and a whole lot more fun, by going karting for a day. Most large towns have kart tracks, often indoors. These are ideal for practising controlled sliding, without the danger of damaging your car, and in a safe environment.

While a severe skid or total brake failure (see page 133) is probably the scariest experience you will have whilst driving a car, suffering a sudden tyre blowout can be almost as bad. Unlike a gradual decrease in tyre pressure, a blowout means that the tyre will deflate instantly. This will cause the car to pull dramatically to the left or right, depending on which tyre is punctured. Grip the steering wheel firmly, gently apply the brakes and bring the car to a halt at the side of the road at the earliest opportunity. Whilst doing this,

After changing gear, put your hand back onto the steering wheel to regain full control.

127

Driving safely in the rain has as much to do with the condition of your vehicle as it has with the way you drive. Most important of all is the condition of your tyres.

Grip is the priority in the wet, so ensure the tyres are in perfect condition. Similarly, check the wiper blades. If these are split or old they will not wipe the windscreen properly, resulting in smeared and blurred glass, which will reduce visibility. This is compounded when driving in the rain at night.

As well as the wiper blades, the condition of the windscreen can affect vision. If it is heavily scratched it should be replaced. A misted up windscreen will also impair visibility. Turn the heater on to clear the windows, as well as the windscreen.

There are ways you can ensure your driving is as safe as possible in wet conditions. Applying the

Change into a higher gear earlier than normal and keep engine revs down to improve grip.

accelerator and brake pedals gently will reduce the risk of the wheels spinning or skidding respectively, while changing up into a higher gear earlier than normal and keeping the engine revs down will improve grip.

It is recommended that in good weather conditions, a two second gap should be kept between your vehicle and the vehicle in front, so in wet weather or when the roads are slippery, leave a four second gap. Do

AUTO ADVICE

In wet weather, ensure your windows are clear and clean. Reduce your speed and stay alert.

Always allow plenty of time to stop – particularly in busy, built-up areas.

the next convenient landmark, until you leave a big enough gap.

Be aware of vehicles behind you as well as in front. If there is a truck following you, its braking distance will be longer than usual in wet weather, so do not suddenly apply your brakes. Watch the road ahead for hazards such as standing water, especially at the side of the road. This will give you ample time to react. Should you drive into deep standing water, or find yourself aquaplaning over water, steer towards where you want to exit, or away from any obstacles.

this by taking note of when the vehicle in front passes a stationary object and counting for four seconds. If you pass the same object before you finish counting to four, slow down, and then repeat the process when you come to

Keep at least a four second gap between you and the traffic in front in wet conditions.

HOW TO DRIVE IN ICY/ SNOWY CONDITIONS

Driving in snow or icy conditions should only ever be undertaken if your journey is essential. All the same procedures apply for driving in such conditions as for driving in the rain.

Driving in snow or ice requires far more concentration and care due to the often unforeseen dangers of the conditions, particularly when so-called black ice occurs. Hard to detect, and a major hazard, this is when water on the road surface freezes, resulting in a layer of ice covering the road. Watch for frozen puddles as a guide.

As with driving in the rain, ensure your windows are clear and clean. You may have to use a scraper or

winter driving dos & don'ts

▶ **DO** tell someone where you are heading and the route you are taking.

▶ **DON'T** start off on your journey until the heater has cleared the inside of the windows properly.

▶ **DO** take a mobile phone and a bottle of drinking water along with you in the car.

▶ **DON'T** forget to pack warm clothes and blankets, in case you get delayed or stuck. In very severe, wintry conditions, consider carrying snow chains and a towrope in the car – make sure you know how to fit the snow chains first.

▶ **DO** follow the advice given on page 126 if your vehicle starts to skid or slide.

de-icer to clear ice or snow from the outside of the glass. Ensure the lights and mirrors are also clear of snow.

Braking distances in ice and snow can be substantially longer than normal, so leave plenty of room between vehicles, control your speed, and use the brakes earlier and more gently. Fresh snow offers more grip

Use a scraper to clear snow and ice from the windscreen before setting off.

than ice, so try not to follow in the tyre marks of vehicles before you. (However, this advice applies only on the road; it can be difficult to judge the depth of heavy snow in rural areas, where following previous tracks may be preferable).

If your car is equipped with ABS (automatic braking system) or traction control, use them. ABS can help prevent the car from skidding by rapidly applying the brakes, similar to cadence braking (page 126). Traction control will help reduce wheel spin by distributing power evenly to all four wheels, providing the car with the best grip. Traction is the most important aspect of driving in severe conditions,

AUTO ADVICE

If in doubt, slow down! Excess speed in slippery conditions is a major cause of accidents on the roads in winter.

so observe the way ahead to find likely areas of the road with the best grip possible.

There are some preparations you can carry out for wintry conditions. Ensure that your car's battery is in good working order, as it will be called upon to work harder; keep your petrol tank full to be able to keep the engine, and hence the heater, running should you get delayed or stuck.

Finally, the onset of winter is a good time to check your car's cooling system for anti-freeze, as well as all the other points covered in Chapter 4.

ABS and traction control is a great asset for driving on the snow and ice.

DRIVING TIPS

REVERSE PARKING MADE EASY

There is a knack to completing the reverse manoeuvre in one movement. We will assume the parking space is on the left hand or near side (so called because it is the side nearest to the kerb) of the road for the purpose of this exercise.

Drive just past the space so that your vehicle is parallel to the car parked in front of the space, and use your left indicator to warn any passing traffic of your intentions [A]. After checking for pedestrians, begin to reverse and turn into the space, aligning the near side rear corner of your car with the front near side corner of the car parked behind the space. Use your door mirrors as well as looking behind you, and watch the passenger mirror in particular, as you will be able to see the kerb in it [B]. Continue to reverse, aiming the rear corner of the car as described above, until the nearside front corner of your car has passed the rear of the car in front.

Now turn sharply into the space, taking care that you do not make contact with the car behind [C]. Look for the kerb in the passenger mirror; when your car is parallel to it, straighten the steering. Reverse or move forward carefully to centralise your car in the space.

WHAT TO DO IF YOUR BRAKES SUDDENLY FAIL

Experiencing brake failure is a very unpleasant – and worrying – thing to happen to any driver. There are a few tips to bear in mind should this unfortunately happen to you.

Above all, try not to panic. If there is space in front of you on the road, pump the brake pedal a few times to see if the hydraulic system will 'pump up'. The reason for trying this is that often air will have entered the system and pumping the pedal can expel it, although the cause will need investigating immediately after stopping.

Should pumping the pedal fail, apply the handbrake gently to prevent the wheels from skidding. If your handbrake is adjusted correctly, you should be able to bring the vehicle to a safe, controlled halt. If there is sufficient stopping distance available, prior to using the handbrake you could also try

brake failure dos & don'ts

- ▶ **DO** move into a lower gear, whether you are driving a manual or an automatic vehicle.

- ▶ **DON'T** panic!

- ▶ **DO** try to move over to the side of the road, if safe to do so, and use your horn to warn other drivers and pedestrians.

changing down through the gears. This will slow the car down, as the engine working against the gearbox will reduce speed through what is known as 'engine braking'.

With any luck, applying a combination of the above methods should bring you safely to a halt. If you are travelling at quite a speed and these techniques are not working, as a last resort you could try to scrub off some speed against a grass bank, a wall or crash barrier, aiming for a soft target to crash into. If at all possible, avoid crashing into other vehicles, but in all cases steer away from pedestrians.

AUTO ADVICE
The moment you realise your brakes have failed, switch on your hazard lights without delay.

SUMMARY

- **Correct driving position**

  Find a seating position that is comfortable and supportive

  Your arms should be slightly bent, hands lower than shoulders

  Headrests should be level with the base of your skull

  Ensure that you can reach the controls and pedals properly

- **Driving awareness**

  Be aware of what other road users are doing at all times

  Take regular breaks on long journeys

  Don't be drawn into road rage situations

  Concentrate on your driving, not on anything else

  Drive to suit the road and weather conditions

- **Car control**

  Steer in the direction of a rear wheel skid

  Practice at track days, rally schools or karting, not on the roads

  Maintain smooth, minimal steering movements

  Keep tyres and shock absorbers in good condition

- **Driving in the rain**

  Keep a safe distance between you and the car in front

  Ensure your tyres and wipers are in prime condition

  Ensure your windows are clear and clean

  Reduce your speed and stay alert

- **Driving in the snow**

  Only undertake essential journeys

  Tell someone where you are going

  Watch for ice and likely slippery spots

  Leave longer braking distances

  Aim for areas of the road with the best grip

- **Reverse parking**

  Use mirrors as well as looking behind you

  Take your time

- **Brake failure**

  Pump the brake pedal

  Gently apply the handbrake

  Use the gears to slow down

  Steer away from people

8

Some car owners want to add extras to their cars either to make them more versatile, more personal to their own particular tastes or simply to improve what is already there. Above all, doing this saves having to spend vast sums of money on the next model up the range.

WHAT WILL OR WILL NOT AFFECT INSURANCE PREMIUMS?

You cannot drive in the UK without at least the minimum third party insurance cover required by law, and although it can seem that insurance companies have you cornered when it comes to paying your premium, there are ways to save money.

Newly qualified drivers and young men have traditionally been high risks for insurers, but did you know that if you opt for the Pass Plus scheme after passing your driving test, many insurance companies will give a discount equivalent to one year's No Claims Bonus immediately, which can mean a saving of up to 35% in some cases? Many companies will also ask newly qualified drivers what their test score was – those with fewer 'minor' fail marks are deemed less of a risk.

AUTO ADVICE

If you do not use your car that often, you may get a better deal on a restricted mileage policy.

Extra bodykits and spoilers may look great, but will definitely add to your insurance costs.

Non standard alloy wheels are a temptation to thieves, which makes your car a higher risk.

Unfortunately, one way to increase the cost of insurance is to add extras to your car. Engine performance modifications will have insurers hiking your premium or even refusing to insure you. Even extras such as non-standard alloy wheels, bodykits, spoilers and fancy paintwork will increase premiums, as such additions make the car more desirable to some, so posing a greater risk to the insurer. You may find the premium will not change but the excess – the amount you pay on any claim before the insurance company pays – will increase. Usually, aftermarket alterations to a vehicle's specification will push the price of insurance up, but manufacturers' options are acceptable.

The onus is always on the car owner to inform the insurance company of any modifications. Ask how your insurance will be affected before deciding on any upgrades. There are specialist insurance brokers which deal solely with modified cars, so check the modified car magazines for details. It is sometimes found that the owner of a seriously modified car poses a good risk, as he or she is likely to take extremely good care of their vehicle and keep it garaged.

As ever, shopping around for a policy can pay dividends. You get a better deal for a car that is garaged, for example. Voluntarily increasing your excess may save money, as well.

insurance dos & don'ts

- **DO** fit a Thatcham-approved alarm, which will make your premium drop.

- **DON'T** make modifications and then not inform your insurance company – they will not pay out after an accident if they find the car has been modified.

- **DO** use the internet to search for a more affordable policy. Visit www.confused.com – it will search numerous insurance websites to find the best premium for you.

137

A large estate car is probably the most useful type of car you could own, simply for the space and versatility, but not everyone wants to drive a large estate every day. However, any car can be made more practical by adding a few well chosen accessories.

A tow bar is one of the most useful additions you can make, as not only can it be used to tow a caravan, but you may also tow a trailer to carry a car, motorcycle or jet-ski, as well as a small box trailer to take garden rubbish to the refuse and recycling centre. Tow bars are also ideal for mounting heavy duty bicycle racks, and all manner of brackets are available to mount other types of rack. There are even racks available that can carry a small motorcycle without the need for a trailer.

Any trailer must display the towing vehicle's registration number and have working lights, brake lights and indicators. If bicycles or a motorcycle on a rack attached to the tow bar obscure the number plate or lights, additional items should be fitted. Trailer lightboards are easily available from motor accessory shops for just such a purpose.

You do not necessarily need a tow bar to fit a bicycle rack, as there is also the option of racks which attach to the tailgate of a hatchback using clips and straps. You may still need a lightboard, though, if your lights or registration number are obscured.

Roof racks are great for increasing luggage space. While some claim to be universal, with most modern cars you will probably have to buy the car manufacturer's own design. Many cars now come equipped with roof

AUTO ADVICE

When carrying loads inside the car, never obscure any part of your windscreen or front door windows.

You can buy various brackets to fit onto a tow bar in order to mount racks for bicycles.

Roof racks or boxes are an ideal solution for carrying extra loads on a journey.

rails to which adjustable racks can be fitted. These racks can be used to fit ski boxes, bicycle racks for carrying bikes vertically, and top boxes. Top boxes are lockable, aerodynamically shaped cases of various sizes up to the length of the car roof.

Roof racks, especially when fully laden, can add considerably to a vehicle's fuel consumption. Also, take care not to exceed the car's maximum load; this will be stated in your handbook. Any load on a roof rack should be secured against movement forwards, backwards and sideways, and should be double checked, as an insecure load will detach itself immediately under heavy braking, accelerating or cornering.

Loads inside the car should be secured as well, and if you cannot see out of the rear window, ensure that you have adequate rear vision in your side mirrors.

Modern cars often come without the need for extra capacity. With removeable or fold-down seats, it is worthwhile getting to know exactly how your seats fold and store to make full use of the space available.

car extras dos & don'ts

▶ **DO** seriously consider purchasing a top box for the car roof if you make lots of journeys with masses of luggage. Visit www.roofbox.co.uk for more details.

▶ **DON'T** forget to buy a lightboard if numberplates and lights are obscured by carrying bicycles.

▶ **DO** make doubly sure before setting off that any additional load on your car is properly secure.

INSTALLING A BASIC CAR STEREO

These days it is almost unheard of for a new car to come without a stereo or In Car Entertainment (ICE) system of some sort, but often they will only be equipped with a radio/cassette player, or on older cars, just a radio.

Most stereos will usually be pretty basic and an upgrade will improve sound quality; you may want to upgrade to a CD player. Changing the headset – the equipment that fits in the dashboard – is one of the simpler DIY tasks you can perform on a vehicle. It is easy to mess up the wiring though, so pay attention to the makers' instructions during fitting.

Before you can fit a new headset you will have to remove the old one [A]. Almost all modern cars use the same method to fit these. A couple of tabs on each side of the headset spring out and hold the unit in a 'cage' inside the dash. Standard radio removal tools are available from accessory shops for this purpose [B], though you could make do with four lengths of coat hanger, pushing one through each of the two holes at each end of the unit to release the tabs. Once the old headset is removed from the dash, disconnect the wiring [C]. There will usually be a

AUTO ADVICE

Connect the new headset up and test it first before securing it in place in the dashboard with the clips.

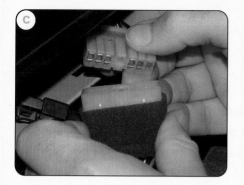

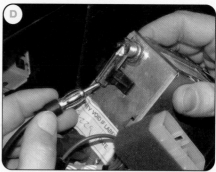

large connector and a smaller one for the speakers, plus an aerial lead.

Depending on the age of your car, it may have industry standard ISO plugs fitted, meaning you can plug the wiring straight into your new headset. However, do not worry if the plugs are different on each unit, as adaptor plugs are available from ICE specialists.

We will assume you are using the speakers that came with the car, as well as any standard amplifier. Using the ISO adaptors means that when you come to re-sell the car, you can simply

stereo installation dos & don'ts

▶ **DO** check if you need adaptor plugs. These connect the power to the new unit directly from your existing plugs; they also connect up to the speaker wires if you are using the standard car speakers.

▶ **DON'T** try and fit expensive or complicated ICE systems yourself. Consult an ICE installation expert.

▶ **DO** pick the right system – reinstalling equipment a week later will waste your time.

refit the original headset using the manufacturer's wiring.

Before the new headset can be installed you will probably have to fit a new cage, as new CD headsets rarely fit older style cages. The cage is the silver open-ended box-type mount that the headset slides into. Release any mounting tabs, remove the old cage, feed wiring through the new cage and slide it into the dash, bending over the mounting tabs to secure it. Do not forget to reconnect the aerial lead [D]. When the security clips on the cage click into place on the headset, it is properly fitted [E].

HOW TO SAVE MONEY ON MOTORING

You can save money as soon as you decide to buy a car by haggling with the salesman (see Chapter 1) or simply opting for a nearly new vehicle, as depreciation of a new car is one of the biggest losses you will experience in motoring.

Downsizing to a smaller car or a smaller engined version of the same model can save money, as can selecting a car that has a low carbon dioxide emissions rating. Vehicle excise duty, or road tax, is based on this and a low CO_2 rating means paying less every year. A diesel powered car may prove even more economical.

Driving gently, rather than frequently burying the accelerator pedal in the carpet, will save on both petrol and wear and tear on mechanical components. Reducing your speed on long motorway journeys, as well as the practice of

AUTO ADVICE

Check the CO_2 rating of any car you are interested in buying: you will pay less in vehicle excise duty for some cars.

saving money dos & don'ts

DO check the internet, both for bargains when buying a car and the best insurance deals.

DON'T neglect your car between services. Regular maintenance could save money in the long run as your car will be less likely to break down.

DO ask to see any old parts that have been removed if a garage carries out any work without consulting you.

car-sharing, will make an even greater difference to your car costs.

Keeping your tyres at the correct pressures reduces fuel consumption, as there will be less drag on the road surface; short journeys are extremely heavy on miles-per-gallon figures, as are traffic jams. Perhaps you do not need to use the car for work if you live reasonably close?

To make substantial savings, you could consider maintaining the car yourself, but only if you feel entirely confident in your abilities.

HOW TO SAVE MONEY ON SERVICING

Every car needs servicing – if only to ensure it has the all-important full service history come re-sale time. But that does not mean you should have to pay through the nose.

If a car is under warranty, you may need to return it to a main dealer for servicing, but still compare prices with different local dealers.

You can save money by doing some of the simple jobs yourself before the service, such as changing any blown bulbs and topping up fluids, which dealers will charge for. Phone around and get quotes from various companies to get the best price. Demand a written set price when you decide on where to take the car, and make the garage aware that you wish to approve any extra work required. For example, when you pick the car up, do not let them tell you that they had to change the brake discs while they were changing the brake pads. If you do find yourself in this situation, refuse to pay for the extra, unapproved work.

The final bill will consist of labour, parts used and consumables. You could try sourcing the parts yourself (they will often be cheaper at a motor parts shop), but main dealers will probably refuse to fit parts other than their own.

If your tyres need changing, you will get the best deal at a dedicated 'quick fit' type outlet.

An independent garage, though, may have no such qualms. Consumables are items such as the fluids – antifreeze, oil and transmission fluid. Replace worn tyres, shock absorbers and exhaust systems at one of the numerous 'quick fit' type centres. These will undoubtedly be cheaper than a dealer supplying the tyres; likewise, with batteries and clutches.

Following your car's service, ask for an itemised bill and query any miscellaneous costs. Check, as far as you are able, that all work you have been billed for has been carried out.

- **Insurance**

  Inform insurance companies of any intended modifications

  Search for the best deals

  Fit a Thatcham-approved alarm

  Never consider driving without insurance

  Make yourself as good a risk as possible to an insurer

- **Making your car practical**

  Roof boxes offer much increased load space

  Tow bars can be used to mount bicycle racks, as well as used for towing trailers and caravans

  Do you need a lightboard?

  When using a roof rack, make absolutely sure the load is secure

  Never overload a roof rack

- **Installing In Car Entertainment**

  Consult the new headset instructions at every stage

  Use the proper tools to remove the old unit

  Check connections – you may need adaptors

  Change cage if required

  Take care with wiring when sliding the new headset into place

- **Save money on motoring**

  Do you need to buy brand new?

  Check insurance group

  Get the best insurance deal

  Check CO_2 ratings and save on road tax

  Drive gently

  Check tyre pressures

  Tackle your own maintenance

- **Save money on servicing**

  Compare dealer/garage charges

  Tackle some simple jobs yourself

  Establish a set price for the job

  Approve any extra work required

  Source your own parts

  Ask for an itemised bill and check through it thoroughly

selling your car

Selling your car can be a stressful business – but it needn't be. There are lots of different ways of achieving your objective, some less painful than others. The main thing is to present your car for sale as well as you can, in order to realise its maximum possible value.

The first impression is all important for any prospective buyer, which means your car's appearance is paramount. Yet many people do not even clean their cars before showing them!

At the very least a car offered for sale should have any rubbish removed from door pockets and the floor, the ashtrays emptied, the carpets and mats vacuumed, and the exterior washed. A car that is clean looks as though it has been cared for, and the simple fact is dirty, scruffy cars are harder to sell.

You could take the car to a professional car valet service or tackle cleaning the interior properly yourself (see pages 86–87), as there are plenty of cleaning products

After a soapy wash, dry the excess water with a chamois leather to eliminate any smears.

Before a potential buyer comes round to view, give your car a thorough wash.

AUTO ADVICE

Clean all those areas that are normally ignored, such as the inside frame of all doors and even the foot pedals!

available. Two areas that are often overlooked when cleaning a car interior, yet can make a big difference to the appearance, are the door shuts (the area by the door hinges, revealing the bodywork when open) and the glass. The latter is especially important if the car has been used by a smoker. It is also a

Clean door shuts suggest to a buyer that the car has been well-maintained and looked after.

If your car has a black bumper, apply special bumper black to restore its worn colour.

preparation dos & don'ts

- **DO** use a paintbrush to remove dust on the trim or rubber before repairing any splits with adhesive.

- **DON'T** bother taking your car to a bodywork specialist and spending lots of money in making good small scratches or tiny dents. See pages 83–85 for advice on sorting them out yourself.

- **DO** remove all clutter from the car.

good idea not to smoke in your car a few weeks before you plan on selling it. Fit an air freshener as well, but take it out before potential buyers view the car. After vacuuming, a paintbrush makes an extremely effective tool to remove dust from dashboard vents.

Moving on to the exterior, after washing the car you may decide to polish the bodywork, apply bumper black to restore faded bumpers and tackle alloy wheels with a proprietary cleaner, all of which can improve the appearance immensely. If your car has plain steel wheels, or the wheel trims are broken or scuffed, consider fitting a set of cheap wheel trims (see below). For the minimal outlay these represent, they can dramatically improve the appearance – and therefore saleability – of a vehicle. Top up the oil and water and check the tyre pressures, as you want the car to drive as well as possible on any test drive.

An old, battered wheel (left) can be dramatically improved by adding a cheap wheel trim (right).

PRESENTATION FOR SELLING

Having thoroughly cleaned the car and made it as presentable as possible, make sure it is readily accessible for when any prospective buyer arrives.

For the viewing, ensure that all the doors are unlocked, raise the bonnet if asked to, remove the keys and leave the viewers to inspect the car. Stay close by but leave them to it, and only start the car or offer a test drive if asked. If they are interested, they will ask to drive the car.

Have all the relevant documentation for the car to hand for inspection: this means, the Vehicle Registration Document, the current MOT certificate, any previous MOT certificates and any vehicle history, such as a service history in the service manual or garage bills. If you have any relevant literature, such as a handbook or manual, include those as well.

When selling your car privately, any prospective buyer will be coming to your home, and there is nothing that will put them off more than seeing a scruffy seller or property, so bear this in mind and dress fairly smartly. When he or she arrives, be friendly and helpful but do not talk too much. Only offer information about the

viewing dos & don'ts

DO make sure your vehicle meets basic levels of roadworthiness. If your vehicle is seriously defective and unroadworthy, you may be committing an offence by selling it.

DON'T allow uninsured test drives. Check test drivers are covered by either your insurance policy or the potential buyer's.

DO ask for ID, if in any doubt, to prove the buyer is who they say they are.

vehicle when asked. Do not arrange for a buyer to come late in the evening – only make appointments that are suitable to you. Preferably, get any enquirer's telephone number, as you will be amazed how many times people fail to turn up after arranging to view a car for sale.

Remember to be aware of your personal safety too, especially when letting a stranger, or even more than one, into your home. It would be prudent to ensure you are not alone when a potential buyer makes an appearance, to be on the safe side.

AUTO ADVICE

Always accompany any potential buyers on a test drive, no matter how honest you think they look!

There are plenty of ways to sell a car, from selling to a dealer for cash, which will return the least amount, to placing an advert in a shop window or paying for an insert in a local newspaper.

Local newspapers carry 'cars for sale' sections and will reach a large audience. Some offer picture ads, which will really show off your car. The best results from printed media come from *Autotrader* or *Exchange & Mart* type publications, which are aimed exclusively at potential car buyers. A photographer will come to your home or workplace to take the picture and collect the advertisement text, making the whole process very easy.

The internet has become a great way to sell cars too, whether by using sites such as e-Bay or by registering with an on-line car database. These charge a one-off fee to register and your car stays on the database until sold; it is matched with people looking for that particular model of car.

Be aware that certain types of car sell more easily, and certainly for more money, at certain times of the year. For instance, no-one wants to buy a convertible in winter, but come the first sunny days of spring, such a

car becomes extremely desirable. The same holds true for sports cars, while 4x4s can fetch more money in winter when it is muddy and icy.

Whichever way you choose to advertise your car, it is important that the advert is worded well. State the exact year, model and mileage – making a point of any low mileage,

Car sections in local newspapers are one of the best places to advertise your vehicle.

AUTO ADVICE

Visit www.glass.co.uk for a price guide to your vehicle, so that you can value your car realistically.

the engine size, whether it has any service history and how long the MOT certificate is valid for. Petrol or diesel engine is an important point, as is the colour. Likewise, if there are any existing warranties, especially those provided by the manufacturer.

Be honest about the condition of the car. Do not forget to include the price and phone number, and state a time period in which to call if you want to avoid feeling you should stay by the phone constantly.

The value of a car is always difficult to ascertain, and will depend on its age, condition and mileage. Many sellers price their cars too high, but you do not want to underprice it either. Check with price guides or look at the local paper.

Probably most tellingly, your car will be compared to similar models advertised alongside it, so check the other prices wherever you are advertising the car. Do not include the term 'offers' or 'ono' (or nearest offer) – any serious buyers will make offers anyway. If the car is priced correctly, the phone will ring, but be patient – the second-hand car market is tough.

People crave tough, reliable 4x4s during the winter months, so this is a good time to sell.

guide to ad abbreviations

F/S/R	factory sunroof
S/R	sunroof
5DR	5 door
G.COND *or* gd con	good condition
VGC	very good condition
exc. con	excellent condition
H.R.W.	heated rear window
P.A.S.	power assisted steering
ALLOYS	alloy wheels
C/L *or* c/locking	central locking
R/WIPE	rear wiper
S/H	service history
FSH	full service history
E/SEATS	electric seats
E.W. *or* e/windows	electric windows
F/FOGS	front fog lights
TINTS	tinted windows
top spec	best specification of the model
a/c *or* aircon	air conditioning

DOING THE DEAL

So you have advertised your car, a potential buyer has come to view it, he or she has inspected it inside and out, and is now keen to take the car for a test drive.

The first rule for any test drive is: do not let buyers do this without you, as you run the risk of never seeing your car again! Drive the car yourself first, so they can see it driven smoothly by someone who is used to it, then let them take the wheel. After the test drive remain in the car and ask if there are any questions. This is important, as you can maintain eye contact and the buyer is contained within an environment that you have control over. After answering any questions, you should ask if they want to buy the car. They have, after all, looked over it, driven it and asked questions about it. When they say 'yes', you can close the deal. Now is the time to get out of the car.

selling dos & don'ts

- **DO** ensure the DVLA is told that the vehicle has changed hands as soon as possible. Don't put it off, otherwise future convictions and offences will be traced back to you!

- **DON'T** sell a car which is subject to a hire purchase (HP) or conditional sale agreement, unless you have the finance company's permission.

- **DO** include any information in your written receipt if you are selling a car for spares only or if the car needs substantial repairs, so you will not get any comeback.

- **DON'T** let a dealer give you a raw deal on your car. If you are not satisfied with his offer, walk away and sell privately.

AUTO ADVICE

It is a good idea to ask a little more than you expect to get, to give you a bit of negotiating room in the deal.

You may be lucky and find a buyer who is happy with both the car and the price. However, most will make an offer and then the two of you start haggling. Use any benefits of your car such as new tyres, an alarm or even the full service history to justify a higher price. Never drop the price before being asked, even if you think it will finalise the sale; let them make the first bid. Having reached this point, you know the buyer is interested in the car, so only reduce the price by small amounts. When you accept any offer make conditions, such as payment in cash or payment that day. Take a deposit if they want to buy the car but do not have the total purchase amount with them. If you cannot reach an agreement on the deal, be polite but firm and tell them to take it or leave it. This way, they may reconsider and will not feel they have lost face if they return.

Never hand over the keys to the car before you have been paid in full. This is important to remember, especially if the buyer pays by cheque. In this instance, keep hold of the car until the funds have cleared in your bank account. If you are paid by banker's draft, telephone the issuing bank to verify its authenticity. Do not stop taking enquiries from other interested parties until you have been paid in full, as this will give you a list of telephone numbers for other potential buyers should this deal fall through.

Once you have been paid in full, you can give the buyer any documentation relating to the vehicle's history, the MOT certificate and the relevant part of the Vehicle Registration Document, as well as a signed and dated receipt. It is a

Never hand over your keys until you are sure the deal has been properly finalised.

criminal offence to fail to notify the DVLA of a vehicle transfer, and you must send the Registration Document back to the DVLA if it was issued after 1 March 1997, or complete the tear-off slip and return that to the address shown on the form if issued before 1 March 1997. The top part of such a form is given to the buyer, who must complete it and also send it to the DVLA. Prompt action here will ensure that you will not become involved if the vehicle is used to commit any offences after you have sold it.

- **Preparing for sale**

  Clean and detail the car for best appearance

  Top up oil and water

  Clean the inside of all windows

  Clean alloy wheels or fit new wheel trims

  Check tyre pressures

- **Presentation for selling**

  Have all documents to hand

  Be helpful and offer information only when asked

  Make the car readily accessible

- **Advertising your car for sale**

  Selling to a dealer offers the worst return

  Try picture adverts in *Auto Trader* magazines or the local paper

  Advertise on the internet

  Advertise at the best time of year if car is a convertible or 4x4

  Clear and honest descriptions work best for selling your car

  Remember to include price and phone number

  Compare prices and advertise accordingly

- **Doing the deal**

  Accompany the test driver

  Remain in the car after the test drive

  Answer questions and ask if they want to buy

  Use benefits of car to justify highest price when haggling

  Take deposit to ensure buyer returns

  Keep keys and documents until full payment has cleared

  Inform DVLA of change of ownership

USEFUL CONTACTS

WEBSITES

www.british-car-auctions.co.uk	auction sales and news
www.confused.com	compare car insurance quotes
www.dvla.gov.uk	Driver and Vehicle Licensing Agency
www.flintinsurance.co.uk	insurance brokers with female-friendly policies
www.glass.co.uk	vehicle prices and running costs
www.hpicheck.com	vehicle history checks
www.motcentrefinder.co.uk	MOT station locator and advice
www.parkingsensors.co.uk	sensors to aid reverse parking
www.passplus.org.uk	bringing insurance down for new drivers
www.rac.co.uk	RAC car data check and inspections
www.roofbox.co.uk	The Roofbox Company. Mail order suppliers
www.smmt.co.uk	Society of Manufacturers and Traders
www.theaa.com	AA car data check and inspections
www.ukaudioshop.com	in car entertainment
www.ukcarcheck.com	vehicle history checks
www.ukmot.com	MOT station locator and advice
www.vsib.co.uk	Vehicle Systems Installation Board
www.vosa.gov.uk	Vehicle and Operator Services Agency

ADDRESSES

Association of British Insurers
51 Gresham Street
London
EC2V 7HQ

DVLA
Swansea
SA6 7JL

VOSA (Vehicle and Operator Services Agency)
Berkeley House
Croydon Street
Bristol
BS5 0DA

ABS (Automobile
Buyers Services)   0800 358 5855

**Consumer Credit and
Trade Association**   01274 390380

DSA
Test enquiries   0870 0102372
Head office   0115 901 2940

DVLA
Driver enquiries   0870 240 0009
Vehicle enquiries   0870 240 0010

Insurance Ombudsman   0845 080 1800

Office of Fair Trading   0345 224499

SMMT (Society of Motor
Manufacturers and Traders)   08457 585350

St John Ambulance   01732 871666

VOSA (Vehicle and
Operator Services Agency)   0870 606 0440
VOSA MOT enquiries   0845 600 5977

VSIB (Vehicle Systems
Installation Board)   01708 340911

GLOSSARY

4x4	Four wheel drive vehicle
ABS	Anti-lock brakes
alternator	Generator providing electricity for the vehicle's electrical system when the engine is running; charges the battery
anti-freeze	Liquid that prevents coolant system freezing in winter and aids summer cooling
battery	A 'power reservoir' that stores electricity
camber	The amount a wheel deviates from vertical, such as on the rear of a VW Beetle
carburettor	Mixes fuel and air into vapour which burns in engine
coolant	Mix of water and anti-freeze
coolant pump	Driven by the engine, it pumps coolant around the cooling system
crumple zone	Part of vehicle structure designed to collapse in an accident, protecting occupants
DSA	Driving Standards Agency
DVLA	Driver and Vehicle Licensing Agency
flooded engine	When neat fuel enters the engine causing it not to start
fuel injection	Injects fuel directly into engine
grey import	Cars sourced from outside the European Union
hard shoulder	Narrow lane on left hand side of motorways to be used in emergencies
HP	Hire Purchase
ICE	In car entertainment
jump start	Using another car's battery to assist starting the engine when the battery is flat
MOT test	Annual roadworthiness test
MPV	Multi Purpose Vehicle
OEM	Original Equipment Manufacturer (manufacturer parts)
parallel import	Cars sourced from inside the European Union

pattern parts	Aftermarket parts that are copies of original manufacturer's parts
PCP	Personal Contract Purchase
PNC	Police National Computer
runners	Part worn tyres
shock absorbers	Suspension dampers which prevent continuous bouncing from suspension springs
SORN	Statutory Off Road Notification
spark plugs	Responsible for igniting fuel/air vapour
SRS	Supplementary Restraint System – airbag
Supermini	Modern small car with equipment previously found on larger, more luxurious cars
SVA	Single Vehicle Approval
Thatcham-approved	Motor Industry Repair Research Centre at Thatcham in Berkshire. Tests and approves security devices
thermostat	Controls the flow of coolant around the engine
traction control	Electronic device which ensures driven wheels do not slip or spin
transmission	General term describing the components used to transmit drive to the wheels, commonly referring to automatic gearboxes
Vehicle Excise Duty	Road tax
VIN	Vehicle Identification Number
VOSA	Vehicle and Operator Services Agency
wheel brace	Special wrench for loosening and tightening wheel nuts
write-off	Insurance terminology for a car too badly damaged or uneconomical to repair

INDEX

INDEX

ACKNOWLEDGEMENTS

The author and publishers would like to thank the following individuals and organisations for their kind help and assistance in providing images for this book:

RAC
AA
DVLA
VOSA
Cartell, Dean Street, East Farleigh, Maidstone, Kent
Coopers of Sevenoaks, Kent
Flint Insurance, High Street, Bexley, Kent
Halfords, Old Otford Road, Sevenoaks, Kent – with special thanks to Nic Baker, Mike Rixon and Darren Robinson
Highways Agency
Kwik-fit, London Road, Sevenoaks, Kent
St John Ambulance – especially Sue Piper
Vauxhall

The publishers would also like to credit the following organisations for the use of their images in the book:

Police Service of Northern Ireland (page 22)
Autoliv (pages 111, 112, 116 and 117 [top])
The Roofbox Company (page 7)